Unbinding the Bondages of the Brain

A Spiritual-Behavioral Approach

J. Paul Briggs

Note: There is a realignment happening in psychotherapy that takes time to materialize. The evidence is indisputable. Psychotherapy has been good at identifying problems but not at correcting them. When there is personal and spiritual renewal however because of the gospel of Jesus Christ and His church, there is not only a transformation of conscience, character, and behavior, but a stark improvement in the individual, society, and culture. Despite the origin and existing field of psychotherapy steeped in an atheistic paradigm, the future for those with mental problems is bright, as greater awareness and common sense sees that science and reason is compatible with and dependent upon The Source of Light.

Unbinding the Bondages of the Brain

Table of Contents

Preface...1

1. Human Nature and Condition................3

2. Psychosis, Phobia, and Addiction........31

3. Treating Dependency...........................45

4. Getting Better.....................................57

5. Firm Resolve to Attain Goals...............73

6. Facing the Fear of Dying......................87

Bibliography...102

Preface

The superlative descriptions of the brain, such as "the amazing brain" or "the magnificent brain" are insufficient. In fact, no words can deservedly describe it and certainly not its importance and significance to one's well-being. If Biblical admonition calls the body to be a holy temple of the Lord, this means that the brain is sacrosanct, being its central command station. Since it controls all human thoughts and behavior, the human brain is more than a most sacred vessel, it is perhaps the most prized possession of its Creator.

We are only beginning to learn about the functions and dysfunctions of the brain. What we should know is that our greatest responsibility is to safeguard it against any unnecessary damage or corruption, and anything that would diminish its effectiveness. The prime culprits of such attacks are the bondages of the brain: *conflict, psychosis, phobia, and addiction,* as well as the *fear* of *dying.* This book offers some insights, spiritual and behavioral rather than chemical, toward dealing with each.

For all those that specialize in the helping professions, nothing can be more important than to realize and convey to others that God is our greatest helper. When one turns away from God, the response to pressures, stresses, and strains of life situations become all the more difficult and overwhelming. The making of immoral choices will occur more readily as well, and of course, will have their own worse consequences.

Unfortunately, far too many therapists dismiss God, and fail to see any connection between the spiritual and psychological. The brain is far too marvelous to miss its relationship to the Creator. Those in a desperate condition perhaps can only succeed and are most likely to, if they realize the wondrous power of God's redemption is available to them. It is not something that should be overlooked in the therapeutic setting.

One can choose either to go toward or away from God and the choice can make a profound difference. If we choose to ignore, deny, or reject God in the process of understanding our life situation, we limit our awareness about who we are; our purpose in life; why we are here; our duty to others; and where we hope to be going now and in the long term. The secret weapon of the most successful therapy often comes down to prayer and forgiveness. The ability of one to put their trust in God and to forgive others for harm done to them and forgive oneself for the harm they have done to others.

God does not put barriers, hurdles, and difficult situations in our lives to hurt us. God is always there to help if one only turns to Him, especially in time of need, and no matter what the situation we find ourselves. God has a reason for the challenges in our life and He will help us through it if we turn our hearts to Him

Chapter 1

Human Nature and Condition

"The flesh wars against the spirit and the spirit against the flesh." (Galatians 5:17) We live in a constant state of internal conflict, it is our human nature and condition. Conflict is a state of opposition or disagreement. A moral conflict or immoral act is when a person knows what they should do or not do according to God's commands, how they should or should not think and behave, but they choose to do otherwise. Acting wrongly or failing to act rightly (omission) is a moral conflict against one's better judgment or conscience.

Bondages of the brain often occur when problems arise due to moral conflict, and they are greatest if they become habitual or extreme. This occurs when one fails to self-correct or be corrected by others, one's parents, teachers, coaches, or the police. Difficulties frequently come about when one becomes insensitive to their own immoral behavior, and it causes damage to others and oneself.

The culture demands tolerance to what are offenses to the dignity of human beings and at the same time celebrates freedom from guilt and moral conflict. In doing so, it perpetuates the degeneration of the moral conscience. The feeling of guilt is essential for the maturing of the moral conscience and morally acceptable behavior. When guilt fails to form in one's conscience, an insensitivity to resultant problems occurs, and serious destruction ensues. The longer corrective action is not taken to align thoughts and conduct in conformity with moral Biblical teachings, for example, the greater is the loss of self-control in individuals and society.

The more desensitized one becomes from immoral behavior, the greater becomes the rationalizations for the behavior. This freezes the conscience, shuts it down, causing the person to become almost immune to self-correction. In the war between what is right and wrong, the calices that form from bad habits and wrong choices harden over by repeated inappropriate rationalizations and conclusions. Rather than dealing with the matter, it leads either to a "fight or flight" response pattern by the individual.

The "fight" response is reflected in destructive behavior toward others through one's obsessive drive for money, power and pleasure, striving for control over others to meet what one thinks are urgent needs. The "flight" response is taken by one who may be sensitive and responsible in nature but cannot seem to find the right path in life. They seem to be running away from reality and look for diversions as a way of not facing what it takes to meet their needs. Whether one has "fight or flight" tendencies because of their contention over moral conflict, the ultimate consequence sometimes leads to psychosis, phobia, and/or addiction.

The Moral Choice

When Jesus said, "I am in this world but not of this world," (John 17:16) He was reminding us not only of His nature, but of our own divine nature and our intended destiny. God wants us to keep our eyes on the miracle of His creation in order to understand why we live and have purpose. The human brain is sacrosanct because it and we are God's creation. We cannot abuse or disregard it so much and so often that we forget its nature and why God made us. He provided us with such a valuable command and control center it forces us to realize we must be intended to be connected to God. Since we are His children, in His likeness and as His protégés, our brains are meant to mirror God. They are to give forth a reflection never intended to be far removed from His light and spirit.

This is why prayer is such a spiritual energizer. It is like plugging the Tesla car into its battery source. This state-of-the-art car cannot move until its battery is charged and then it becomes a thing of beauty. The brain works best when it is activated and connected to its source, God the Father, its Creator. Anyone who studies the brain realizes that it could not have come from nowhere or from some random evolutionary development. It obviously was and is a special gift from a Supreme Creator. And as this is so, wouldn't it be a good idea to check in every now and then just to say thanks?

Conflict occurs when one's basic outlook on life is self-serving, the "world view" that believes everything revolves around me, and every action is to satisfy and protect me. God wants us to have the "complete view," that everything comes as a gift from God, and we are dependent upon Him. From this view, we want to give freely to others for we see God's love for us. The "world view" is a slave to self-possessiveness, selfishness, and death; the "complete view" is free to love, is generous to others, willing to sacrifice, and sees eternal life as the goal.

Jesus said, "the good tree will bear much fruit and the rotten tree will be thrown in the fire." (Matthew 7:19) People can be attracted to the world view but it minimizes one's sense of divine purpose. In following the world view, one abandons their own true nature designed to follow the well-lit path. When our thoughts and actions do not square with how we innately know we should be, we put a halt to real problem-solving, to real discovery and understanding of self, and to real personal growth and freedom.

Where there is a life that is stuck in relativism and hedonism, there should be a person in intense anxiety and frustration as it is entirely contrary to one's true nature. One can escape God's light with temporary diversions but in the darkness of the spirit, one cannot resolve the conflict, discomfort, and guilt. A person can become further detached from the light of life and more desensitized by keeping company with others who live equally under false rationalizations about their own existence. To live in this state, one must fight their mind, will, and soul constantly for such actions will feel incompatible to their true self.

Conflict begins as an internal fight within the mind. St. Augustine of Hippo, who lived from 354 to 430 A.D., stated the obvious a long time ago, "the mind cannot rest until it rests in God." (Book 1, Chapter 1 of *The Confessions*) Conflict within an individual and between people is often only able to be resolved once we understand that we are His…each a child of God. It is often difficult to reconcile the secular world view from the Great Command to love God and neighbor as self. The latter comes with the highest motive to know, love, and serve God. The "culture of death" has a natural corrosive impact on the mind, will, and soul. It must be rejected in order to meet our true needs, and unfortunately today, that secular world view mentality dominates the culture.

Keep in mind for a moment the goal of the evil one, the devil, Satan, the dark spirits, call it whatever. If our brain is the sacred tool God gave us to use to meet every challenge life presents, then be sure that the secular world view, the culture of death, the evil one, seeks most of all to destroy this holy vessel that provides the natural innate divine bond with the Creator, that connects God to all His creation. There is going to be a non-stop war of evil trying to outdo good and the primary target is the brain.

We know that good has the power to win out over evil. (Romans 12:21; Proverbs 11:17; John 3:16) But the simple fact is we must choose good, or the power of evil does win. That is, one must know that evil cannot win if one turns to God, but it can win out if one does not turn to God. The culture of death does all it can to deceive, diminish and reject God, and creates hardship for anyone striving to meet their true needs. The battle for the soul is a struggle the brain can win. It a war between the "culture of life" versus the "culture of death" and it must be recognized for what it is; ***moral conflict*** that must be won.

When we look for hope in the world, the secular world view often produces pessimism that can lead to depression, disorientation, and confusion (**psychosis**). When one seeks a new safe reality within one's own mind through a turning inward, and isolates themselves from others, they enter a world of delusions, and become stuck in a frozen, immobilized state. It can be a place of deep anxiety and depression, a catatonic shut down. All of this and the entire process is the broad definition of psychosis which begins with mental trauma and often moral conflict.

The secular world often provokes fear in many forms and on many matters, from various high alerts to dangers issued from science reports to seemingly life-ending weather forecasts. The hidden intent is a subtle injection of the power of the world over our God-given nature, almost intended to invoke fear, loss of control, and loss of faith (**phobia**). That is, if one lets fear enter one's mind and control it, one forgets what we should instinctively know, that God is always there to strengthen and sustain us. (Isiah 40:29; Romans 16:25-27) It is important to pay attention to the cautions of the secular world but to realize that it sometimes is an overreaction due to a disbelief in

God and a sense that everything depends on them, as if they are in control and responsible for what goes on.

Moreover, when one comes under stress, is frustrated by life, is failing to find success or attain goals, is perhaps demeaned by others, one should turn to God, but so often instead runs away from Him and flees to substance abuse (**addiction**). It can come in the form of some compelling false fulfillments such as the quest for money, power, or pleasure as well, or anything that might keep one busy and occupied with work or some form of obsessive-compulsive habits of diversion from reality. All these bad choices arise from a lack of faith and an avoidance of God.

The Burdens of the Brain

The underlying source of so many types of **psychosis, phobia, and addiction** is the tension created when we are at odds with our true nature. This internal pressure is increased, and problems exaggerated when one tries to hide it from others and is not open to discussion about it. The tendency in therapy is to focus on the abnormal behavior rather than the source of the problem, the moral conflict and bad choices being made to address the real issues.

Moral **conflict** is often the root cause that underlies many, though not all, problems of the mind. When it does, the contention between good and evil and the choice one chooses should be the focus. It is a classic struggle over inclinations toward what one knows one *should* think and do opposed to what one has done, is doing, or wants to do.

This conflict causes the brain not to function the way it should. The choice to ignore good and follow evil or to reject one's true God-centered spirit in favor of the evil spirit is the start of most personal problems.

Conflict when uncorrected or left unaddressed can cause personal confusion, fear, and produce many bad habits. The consequences of such may seem small and insignificant at first, but when ignored leads to serious issues and often mental problems.

Sometimes the conflict begins when one thinks there is no such thing as the devil or evil spirits. Self-deception about the reality of evil spirits is the shortest path to self-destruction. Where there is the denial that evil exists, then these spirits have free reign over the individual. Once open to demonic abuse, the individual is ripe for being led down the path to all sorts of psychoses, phobias and addictions.

Often just letting a person talk out their thoughts with someone willing to listen, a person with a firm belief in God will eventually be enough to bring them back to wholeness again. It takes a clearing of the evil influence that has control of one's conscience to recover a true and complete sense of self, that sense that reaches to God and says: "I need You." Anyone wanting to talk to God will find answers as He always will listen and respond. (Matthew 6:6; Luke 18:1-8)

Whenever a soul is searching for God, help is on the way. The Alcoholics Anonymous 12 Step Program (a replica of the Catholic confession) starts with the acknowledgement of God and our powerlessness over evil without Him. It takes humility of spirit to begin to understand this important fact, and from something as simple as this emanates the greatest form of human healing. It is the same healing that has been around for thousands of years, long before the dawn of human psychology and psychiatry and anti-psychotic medicines for every form of anxiety. It is likely that whenever faith in God declines, visits to the psychologists, psychiatrists, and the allocation of medicines increase. The two work best in tandem; where there is acknowledgement of God as a vital part of the helping process.

The Response to Individual Needs

There is nothing more important than responding appropriately to the conditions in our life that we encounter. Meeting our own true needs ironically focus not so much on self, but on God and others. Every day we encounter the reality of choice, between selfish desires or the meeting true needs, that is, in the giving and living for oneself versus living for the love of God and others. The first leads to a worldly wealth that enslaves and does not last; the latter provides richness in spirit and freedom that is fulfilling and lasts forever.

God gave us brains that must reflect their creator. That is, they are designed to respond to His wishes, doing what He wants us to do, fulfilling His mission in our lives, bringing love to all His creation. All decisions that lead us off the track of doing the next right and loving thing fail to meet our true needs, which must reflect what God wants of us. It may seem harmless or meaningless, but each step down the wrong path is a step away from God, an opportunity lost, an offense to the very nature of the brain God gave us.

God gave us a "free will" and we constantly make choices to do right or wrong, good or evil. We choose to learn from mistakes or deceive ourselves about our true needs. We may be helped or hindered by one's upbringing, background and environment, and one's own unique situation. We may be molded in a healthy or unhealthy way by life's experiences. We may see clearly or be blinded by others, being positively or negatively impacted. In the end, it's up to us to choose our thoughts, words, and deeds, and decide to live in a manner compatible with our God-given nature, or not. We all have the same true needs coming from the same One who made us, who is constantly calling us back to Him, but we choose whether or not to listen and respond.

The "general human condition" relates to the fact that we are all people with common needs living in the world striving to meet these needs. The question of greatest importance is one's understanding of what those common needs are and what is the best way to meet them. There are true needs, those that tie to the Greatest Commandment to love God and others as self, and there are false needs, such as the delusion that striving for money, power, and pleasure are critical toward meeting one's needs. How one defines and responds to needs makes all the difference in life.

One's interpretation of needs consists of two basic choices in life. One is "constructive" and leads to meeting true needs, and the other is "destructive" and does not; instead, it follows an entirely different path that ends at what might be considered "a snake pit." One path leads to God and in doing what we know we "should do" in our lives and toward others (with the help of Divine Aid). The other buys into the devil's empty promises to satisfy selfish motives (with the help of Demonic Aid). Only the constructive path meets the needs of the full person, including the body, mind, soul, social and emotional needs.

"Divine Aid" enables us to clearly "assess, improve, and develop" incrementally toward a person of increasing goodness. "Demonic Aid" leaves us feeling "alienated, impatient, and deceived," often leading one into a cycle causing destruction to oneself and others. The type of spiritual "aid" we choose, whether from God or the devil, makes all the difference in responding appropriately to the general human condition. The path we choose leads one onto a cycle that often becomes somewhat self-perpetuating, one leading to good results and the other often quite the opposite.

The Constructive Path (and Cycle)

Divine AID allows us to "assess, improve, and develop" in a way that is clearly centered on God and the concern for others. The dynamics of this "aid" are as follows:

- *A*ssess: Assesses Needs Properly, Develops Plans, and Makes Wise Choices

- *I*mprove: Analyzes Stress, Makes Assertive Response, Attains Goal, and Reduces Stress

- *D*evelop: Resolves Problems, Meets Needs, and Processes Feedback for Further Improvement

Assess: Divine AID lays the groundwork for the fulfillment of needs. It begins with the willingness to look objectively at ones situation and direction and make an accurate self-assessment. It holds patiently to the promise of eventual success when the right plans and choices are made.

Improve: Improving means correcting even as stress is faced and action plans don't go as smoothly as hoped when they meet reality. One's attitude toward stress, mistreatment and injustice can either be a positive or negative energy source. It can help direct an individual more strongly toward the path of improvement and fulfillment of needs or can lead one down the road to destructiveness. To fulfill true needs we must be assertive, that is in a manner appropriate to attain goals, reduce stress, resolve problems, and fulfill needs.

Develop: The feedback received will enable those in this chosen path to eventually meet true needs as subsequent actions will improve and be ever more refined. Goal attainment provides enough positive reinforcement that it serves to perpetuate the dynamic of success. Success strengthens attitudes and performance toward future success. Failure is averted by having a clear concept of true needs and personal resolve to not be distracted during the quest to meet these needs. One's moral conscience provides feedback that will restore one back onto the right track when improper choices are mistakenly made. When progress is temporarily halted, one becomes determined to adapt for the long haul and redirects oneself based on the meeting of true needs.

The Destructive Path (and Cycle)

Demonic AID leaves one feeling "alienated, impatient, and deceived" and unable to reach one's God-given potential. The dynamics of this "aid" are as follows:

- *A*lienated: Misreads Needs, Fails to Plan, Makes Bad Choices

- *I*mpatient: Fears Stress, Makes Aggressive or Diversionary Response, Pursues Displaced Goals, Increases Stress

- *D*eceived: Fails to Process Feedback Accurately, Needs Remain Unmet, and Problems Increase

Alienated: When overcome by stress, one loses track of true needs and quickly displaces the search for their fulfillment with other selfishly driven goals. With Demonic Aid, one gets "turned off" and decides rather than doing what one knows is right, or should do, instead one does whatever one wants. When ignoring or refusing to realize the nature of one's true needs, temptations of the devil strengthen against oneself. Following this path leads to alienation from God and one's own true self, and it does not abate until one's moral conscience and sense of guilt comes into focus. Only then can repentance, healing and corrective action take place, and if not, a callous disregard for God's way develops.

Impatient: Another characteristic of those that buy into the prompting of the devil is the inability to calmly assess a situation and make proper choices at the right time.   That is, if we do not seek out the advice of our guardian angel, we will not follow God's prompting. Instead, we become overpowered by stress, and react quickly in fear to prevent, minimize, or divert it from us and onto someone else. This reaction is almost always inappropriate and leads to further wrongs being done. Out of fear we run away from the challenge to all sorts of diversions rather than confronting it directly; or confront it directly in a destructive manner of blaming others for our actions.

Deceived: The third characteristic of one choosing the wrong path is that of self-deception. While one thinks they are cleverly deceiving others, the only one they are deceiving is themselves. Over time, their problems can become so severe, they appear to be self-perpetuating; the individual cannot pull free from their own destructive force. When an individual becomes entrenched within a problem cycle, such as with addiction, they are almost entirely unable to use objective information to correct themselves. They have become completely overwhelmed and blind to their true needs. Repentance helps one find hope in God and is the surest way out of this destructive cycle.

Implications for Individual Therapy

Once we have eliminated the possible medical and physiological influences that might cause a problem leading to psychosis, phobia, or addiction, the next proper focus should be on the nature of moral conflict. That is, the next step should be to explore with the individual the cause, origination, and continuation of their problems to determine if the moral choices that have been made are the source of the problem. Is there some unrepentant and unceasing moral conflict in one's life situation?

Modern therapy and academia in general, has largely ignored the integrated approach of treating the mind and soul together. This is simply due to the growing prevalence of political correctness and secularism in the culture that has come to influence these professions that help with mental health problems. Ironically, other than in recent history, for thousands of years the focus on the spiritual dimension of the individual had always been the source and foundation for helping anyone. No longer does it make perfect common sense to start with whether what troubles someone has a moral basis. The matter of what is right and wrong in a moral sense is often considered "private," and addressing such is simply not considered "professional."

Understanding the human condition and the connection between the mind, body, soul, and emotions has been accepted as essential since the times of early Grecian philosophy. Meeting true needs necessitates involvement of the whole person, including the spirit. And while we would like to think of ourselves as self-sufficient individualists, our emotional and spiritual wellbeing is dependent upon our relationship to God and our concern for others.

The essential prerequisite for the truly integrated self rests in the individual's understanding God's love for us and responding to Him in a spirit that highly regards all His creation. By spiritual design, then, others' needs are really our own. We need to show our concern and love for others; this comes from God and is needed to meet our true needs. The fulfillment of human needs purposively includes this "social" dimension whereby only through a unity of spirit and mutual concern for others can one transcend selfish desires.

A Choice for the Good

Each of us goes through a process involving self-assessment, planning and goal setting, and making a choice of action and we do it all the time even when we are unaware of it. It is a part of daily life. Awareness of our true needs during this process helps us make the right choices at the start of this critical path. The truly integrated person is at peace with God and others and keeps this their priority in all their planning and goal setting.

When one responds to God's will, life is never too stressful, nor too difficult, as He never gives anyone more than they can handle with His help. (2 Cor. 1:9) We are an instrument to fulfill His wishes for our lives and those of others; His is a plan much better than any plan made entirely on our own. When calling on God in assessing needs, planning options, making choices, and encountering stress, there is a much greater chance than not that one will respond appropriately.

"Failing to plan is planning to fail" is a very true statement first made famous by Benjamin Franklin. Of course, the clearer the plan, the more it will propel one forward into action. The planning process leads one to continuous improvement. In planning, the self-assessment must maintain maximum objectivity if it is to be effective and the actions that follow successful. Plans encompass both far-reaching vision and detailed day-to-day tasks. Plans motivate and channel energy toward an inspired higher level of performance.

Winston Churchill once said, "the only thing we have to fear is fear itself." Indeed, the thought of stress sometimes induces a fear to respond appropriately. In such cases, the thought of making plans and choices might cause more stress, and thus one retreats into inaction. The failure to act can be disastrous, which would have been the case in Churchill's time.

Courage is working through the fears and stress, but often it is only through one's trust in God that strength is found. The full and honest review of options gives greater insight into what is the best choice but it must always include true needs that incorporate one's spiritual and emotional concerns. The one that pursues the constructive path, properly assesses life's stresses, corrects and improves one's actions, and develops as a fully integrated individual, closely aligned with God and neighbor.

On the other hand, when failing to identify the right goals and plans because we have not included God, sooner or later, internal conflict will set in. Without adequately assessing true needs, our plans and options will not lead us to find happiness and meet life's challenges. One sure sign of this is when behavior deteriorates with unnecessarily aggressive or diversionary responses to stress. A pattern of such behavior only leads one into greater problems and stress. That is, the tendency to "fight" or seek "flight" results in the lack of resolution of problems and stress, and the growing complication of those problems, further intensifying stress.

Fundamental change begins with individual awareness, acceptance, acknowledgment of one's dependence upon God, and gratitude for God's love and protection in our lives. Repetitive failure in life comes from feeling alienated from God, being impatient with others, and deceiving oneself about the outcomes of one's detachment from God and the true needs of self and others.

The paths following Divine AID and Demonic AID are circular in flow, where success begets success, and failure begets failure. The failure to succeed is often not from the lack of effort or will power, but from an insufficient assessment of needs and an inadequate processing of information pertinent to one's true needs. It often comes down to a general lack of gratitude for one's own existence and purpose in life.

As mentioned above, the difference in paths spells the difference in either continuous improvement or continuous failure. Failure can be converted to success at any time through an awareness, acknowledgment, and gratitude of God's existence in our lives. Redemption comes swiftly following repentance. When failing to learn from mistakes however and being deaf to honest feedback, choosing the correct solution is difficult.

The force toward material gain, power, or pleasure or other "goal displacement" objectives is sometimes insidious and almost unconscious to the individual struggling to meet life's demands. Instead of striving to meet true needs, goal displacement sets a life course toward a different direction, and the process usually begins with the rejection or neglect of God and His path for one's life. The stronger this rejection or neglect, the greater is the fuel for goal displacement and the self-destructive problem cycle, that is, the continuous improper response to the general human condition and the mounting problems caused by not acknowledging one's true needs.

One's belief in God affects how one approaches the general human condition of human life. Choosing the moral path, we realize that "doing the next right and loving thing" (Romans 12: 21) for the sake of God and neighbor is what meets our true needs. Conflict arises when one repeatedly fails in this realm due to selfish tendencies and the indifference toward God and others. (James 4:17) In such a state of mind, when encountering severe stress or difficulty in life, this conflict between right and wrong, good and evil, can lead to bad decisions, confusion, fear, and bad habits, that can become the basis for psychosis, phobia, and addiction.

How we respond to the general human condition determines the process and outcomes in our lives, and we respond based on our beliefs or lack of beliefs or false beliefs. Only one path leads to new life; the alternatives to destruction of self and others.

Picture a pyramid divided into several horizontal layers. The lowest and largest area is that of conflict, next up is confusion, then the third rung is fear, and the apex is bad habits. This top layer is the behavior that comes from much conflict, some confusion, and a little bit of fear. This mixture generates bad habits that produce the bondages of the brain. The longer they exist and go uncorrected, the greater the problem. It results in an insensitivity towards, or ignorance of, or belief in falsehoods and untruths about what will be the outcome of present behavior, that is, future consequences become obscured.

As mentioned before, bad habits proceed to great misdeeds if not corrected by one's family, by others, or oneself. Today, this path of destruction is fomented by the culture of death, which has many rationalizations for the evil within it. At the same time, there is an insufficient counter-cultural voice where clergy and religious voices are not heard. This has become a time in history where political correctness turns rightful thinking upside down, where evil is promoted as good, and good as evil, and laws are passed to uphold immoral behavior and confused logic.

The Danger Zone

When one willingly wades into the deep end of a pool, it is not long before the water is up to the neck or over one's head. The danger of being in the deep end is quickly made clear when breathing becomes impossible. You can learn to swim in the danger zone and survive as long as you can manage to keep afloat but that will not be forever. You will eventually need to seek relief and get out and breathe the air God intended for you.

Those that decide to go on the path of self-destruction and associate with those like-minded in thought and group identity, do so at their own risk. Upon accepting a Demonic world view and becoming a member of a group formed by common perspective, one enters a closed society where the stronger the group association, the greater is the self-deception and destructive force within oneself and toward those they oppose.

When firmly fixated within the Demonic world view, one becomes absolutely sustained by group identity, locked into the "destruction dynamic," through a subculture of like-minded members. Their mutual commitment is to "displaced goals" other than their true needs. Their free will becomes less important than sustaining bonds to each other. This mind-set precludes the search for objective truth and corrective action. The prerequisite for one's initiation and continuance in such a group is based upon giving up the right to independent thinking. One's true God-centered needs are suppressed.

The more alienated, impatient, and self-deceived, the greater the chance for Demonic group initiation and the stronger the group bonds. The progression toward destruction for those choosing the Demonic path proceeds in stages from the rejection of God (stage one) to the identification with others who have a similar attitude (stage two), to the response through acts consistent with one's views (stage three). Each stage requires more energy and commitment.

Individuals deeply entrapped by the demonic path must be rescued and removed from the totally seductive demonic forces and review the source for why they have become "alienated, impatient, and deceived." They then need time to be allowed to heal spiritually, emotionally, psychologically and socially through a closely supervised decompression period.

The two students of the Columbine attack, for example, had different personalities and roles, one the leader and one the follower, but were united by a common cause, held a common attitude and commitment to goals, received confirmation from each other as they plotted together to carry out the killing of their fellow high school students. With positive reinforcement to each other and common goals, the two fulfilled their objectives like any other deviant subculture group does. They schemed together (acquiring knowledge, guns, ammunition), mentally rehearsed how their evil deeds could be carried out (thinking through possible scenarios), and then shut down outside influences that might change the course of their planned action (pushing away or rejecting feedback as to their deviate behavior). That is, the only way they could stop themselves would have been to be open to listening to others outside their subculture or being around more normative behavior for some reasonable amount of time, behavior that does not reject them.

Once these individuals failed at self-correction and family and school and community failed in realizing and acting to help stop them, they became an imminent danger. Once deeply in this committed state, they could move quickly from "plan" into "action," based on any number of types of "trigger reactions" to stress or rejection from their environment.

What do the many incidents of violence, such as the Columbine disaster, or the Oklahoma City bombing, or the Mohammed/Malvo sniper incident, or radical Islamic terrorism, or abortion, or teen suicide, have in common? They all reflect a lack of respect for life and a loss of hope. Life loses individual meaning when it is no longer strongly anchored by fundamental values commonly codified in basic Judeo-Christian faiths, and in some interpretations of the Islamic faith. Believers of these faiths must ensure that the culture, including government laws, meet certain moral objectives. When faith itself becomes the impetus, such as when Moslem extremists use the concept of jihad to justify killing innocent non-believers, the rationalization for evil and disrespect for life become so monstrously distorted that a higher authority must intervene.

When the value of life and love of God and others are not preserved and protected by government, individuals and whole cultures, lose their sense of purpose and their spiritual connectivity to God and others. This progresses into the rapid decline and breakdown of family, church, and community. A byproduct of this is an increase of those afflicted with mental enslavements of conflict, confusion, fear and addiction.

The Brain's Pathways

When we form bad habits the neurons of the brain form a clear and strong physiological pathway that leads to the reinforcement of the same thoughts and behaviors. The good news is that God made the brain able to change based on our will. We get to decide what our brain triggers in us. We control it; it doesn't control us. Our free will changes the brain based on what we decide.

Picture a path through the woods that leads to a dangerous situation, maybe to a snake pit. The path no matter how treacherous at first, will become worn and barren if walked on over and over. It is a risky and unsafe path, but after a while it becomes an easy walk as the brush thins out, and one can quickly travel it right to the snake pit.

The brain has neural pathways that are developed by what we think and do, and by what we allow to enter through the senses, the eyes, ears, and even the mouth, nose and via one's sense of touch. Neural pathways have memory cells that quickly develop around past (or desired imaginary) experiences. Once the experiences become habitual, these neural pathways become hard wired connections right to those locations that tend to take control over one's rational thought, where one can fall into the equivalent of a snake pit.

The good news is that God gives us the power to control our life situation. He gave us free will. He gave us a powerful robust brain. The free will is used to chart out a new path in life when we find out a previous path leads to perdition or an unhealthy end. When one replaces bad habits with good habits, the old path that leads to the snake pit gradually grows back its thick brush; the neurons of the destructive neural pathway become redirected to support the new healthy way to live. Internal controls are established so one can live a quality life as God intended.

We live in the present; the past is over. The pain of the past or fear of the future does not need to enter the present time. We decide. If change is needed to build a constructive path, God and the brain He made for us can provide the way. We choose our spiritual AID; it is the choice between good and evil. There is a real difference, and it has real consequences. God gives us power over the evil spirit; we just need to reach out to God for His saving grace.

Someone once said, the goal of life is the process. We create our own processes that lead to a fruitful or not so productive life. Our God is orderly and when we chose to abide in His nature, life is peaceful by design. It is also fruitful and productive, caring and loving of family and others, particularly those with the greatest needs. Find processes and paths in life that lead to good ends and life will be worthwhile. Avoid the paths that lead to mental and actual snake pits.

Moral conflict (sin), confusion (psychoses), fear (phobias) and bad habits (addictions) have physiological, psychological, and behavioral impacts on one's well-being. Corrective action begins with an examination of the facts with a moral conscience and a determination to uproot the source of the problem. Compliance to the Ten Commandments and commitment to God's greatest commandment to love and to the virtues that sustain us, one comes to realize that pride is overcome by humility; greed by generosity; envy by love; anger by kindness; lust by self-control; gluttony by faith and temperance; and sloth by zeal.

Motivation to change comes from realizing that we are all called to be true to ourselves finding God's unique mission for our lives that allows us to know, love, and serve Him and others for His sake. He gave us this magnificent instrument, the brain, to help us do this. He wants us to take care of it and use it to meet our true needs.

Pursuing this goal with clarity of focus, helps us overcome the stresses of the general human condition and avoid the enslavements and bondages of the brain that can easily weigh us down. The nature of these difficulties needs to be understood and that is the subject of the next chapter.

Chapter 2

Psychosis, Phobia and Addiction

The bondages of the brain often begin with a betrayal of the heart, where a mental, physical, and/or sexual abuse is perpetrated upon someone who has close ties to the individual, such as a family member, a relative, a friend, or a trusted authority figure. It can also begin with the shocking loss of someone close to an individual or because of a sudden unexpected injury or affliction. It can occur simply by a chance occurrence, an acting upon one's curiosity, whereby a drug happens to have a very attractive physiological draw.

The destructive cycle begins when one buys into the confusion, fear, and/or bad habit through an act of free will. That is, the cycle continues when one is unable to break away from the self-perpetuating nature of the dangerous path that leads repeatedly to the snake pit of mental health problems, to the inability to meet basic needs, and to the damaging relations with others. The longer one stays on the path, the wider and more worn it becomes. The neural pathway grows stronger over time and develops into a network that connects directly to the brain centers that keep one coming right back to the destructive path. That is, the destructive path develops tributaries that feed into the main neural path. These include malevolent thoughts and wishes, memories of past experiences, as well as places, associates or friends that can lead to trouble.

The kinds of trouble bad habits can lead to are not just with the law but with virtually every aspect of one's existence and one's relationships. When repeatedly ignoring what is right and good to do what is wrong and evil, one will eventually encounter confusion (that can lead to psychoses), fear (that can lead to phobias) and bad habits (that can lead to addictions). As mentioned before, each of these results in physiological, psychological, and behavioral impacts on one's well-being.

Psychosis is defined by The National Institute of Mental Health (NIMH) as:

> a term used to describe conditions that affect the mind, where there has been some loss of contact with reality. During a period of psychosis, a person's thoughts and perceptions are disturbed and the individual may have difficulty understanding what is real and what is not. Symptoms of psychosis include delusions (false beliefs) and hallucinations (seeing or hearing things that others do not see or hear). Other symptoms include incoherent or nonsense speech, and behavior that is inappropriate for the situation. A person in a psychotic episode may also experience depression, anxiety, sleep problems, social withdrawal (e.g., catatonia is one form where the individual does not interact

or react to others), lack of motivation and difficulty functioning overall.[1]

NIMH explains further:

There is not one specific cause of psychosis. Psychosis may be a symptom of a mental illness, such as schizophrenia (characterized by confused or unclear thinking) or bipolar disorder (also named manic-depressive illness), but there are other causes, as well. Sleep deprivation, some general medical conditions, certain prescription medications, and the abuse of alcohol or other drugs, such as marijuana, can cause psychotic symptoms.[2]

During the neural communication between sensory input and mental interpretation of this input, something has gone awry for those experiencing psychosis. When a physiological reason is not found, the goal is to isolate and correct the matter at its source, which has led to the distorted input and interpretation. Often this is a problem with not making the best choices in our thoughts and actions.

There may be environmental, chemical, and biological causes or influences beyond the individual's control or there may be certain moral choices that need to be changed to correct the confusion. That is, if a person has

---

[1] The National Institute of Mental Health (NIMH) website.
[2] Ibid.

made choices that have caused them to be in severe conflict with what they know is right, their ability to think clearly and act normally may be impaired. This takes time to sort through but when addressed properly, the individual can come clean, take ownership, make a full confession, make amends, and go back to their life more determined than ever to do better. This is often the case when a moral conflict has been fully acknowledged and repented.

Phobia is defined by The American Psychiatric Association as follows:

> A phobia is a persistent fear of an object or situation in which the sufferer commits to great lengths in avoiding, typically disproportional to the actual danger posed, often being recognized as irrational. In the event the phobia cannot be avoided entirely, the sufferer will endure the situation or object with marked distress and significant interference in social or occupational activities. As the sufferer approaches a phobic stimulus, anxiety levels increase.[3]

> Social phobia is the fear of other people or social situations such as performance anxiety or fears of embarrassment by the evaluation and scrutiny of others, and may be of a general or specific nature, or even manifest psychosomatic

---

[3] American Psychiatric Association (2013), *Diagnostic and Statistical Manual of Mental Disorders (5th ed.)*, Arlington: American Psychiatric Publishing, pp. 190, 197–202.

symptoms. People with social phobia have extreme feelings of self-consciousness built into powerful fear. Specific phobias is the fear of a single specific panic trigger such as spiders, snakes, dogs, wind, water, heights, flying, catching a specific illness, and people with the phobias specifically avoid the entity they fear.[4]

There are literally hundreds of types of specific phobias. Almost any person, place or thing or experience can be the object of fear because of the irrational nature of such fear. The severity of the fear differs by individual, partly because some fears can simply be avoided, while other fears render the individual powerless to override their panic reaction. The fear can lead to a loss of control, panicking, and even fainting. It is important to understand that fear is a learned behavior, and all learned behavior can be unlearned. The behavior can be learned from first-hand experience, or from watching others reacting fearfully, or hearing information that is believed to threaten one's safety.

The greater the trust in God, the greater ability to quiet and still the mind. For only in God is there true peace and deliberate power over fears. Without a sense of God, a true belief in the very presence of God, one can be subject to any number of fears.

These fears, and there are even many more, all come with strong chemical and physiological reactions. To

---

[4] Ibid.

each person, the sensation is real and very threatening. Psychological desensitization exercises are needed to begin the path to a more peaceful coexistence with one's environment. What is even more important is faith and trust in God, for He is the one who strengthens us, and there is nothing that can defeat Him. "We can do all things through God who strengthens us!" (Philippians 4:13). With the grace of God and through desensitization practice and exercises, one can have the courage to overcome every fear.

Addiction is the repetitive use of a substance or is a compulsive behavior that is dysfunctional toward one's health and fulfillment. This might be substances such as tobacco, alcohol, "street drugs," or prescription drugs, or might include behaviors such as excess gambling, consumption of foods and treats, overuse of the Internet, cellphones, playing of video games, pornography or sex-related indulgences, and sports or fantasy team addictions. In many respects, addiction is anything that is taking over one's life and has become someway dysfunctional to meeting true needs.

To resist any type of addiction temptation, one must first consciously decide ahead of time not to engage in the addiction, and to substitute a positive appropriate action in place of a negative inappropriate action. Planning a good, productive, and fruitful action in place of a bad, counterproductive, and wasteful action; and deciding what is right to do with one's time as opposed to what is wrong, is a necessary first step toward constructive change and improvement.

Once we conceive of a clear and positive path to pursue and begin to develop good habits, the challenge becomes one of maintaining the will to continue on the right path. The problem is that once we submit to the immediate pleasures of the "wrong substance or behavior," the brain chemicals rush to get in the way of thinking rationally and clearly based on reason. This is what is meant by the "physiology of addiction."

Today with the aid of technological breakthroughs and better understanding of the brain, those under the spell of addiction can develop the resolve needed to break through that wall of knee-jerk stimulus-response relapses into addiction. That is, to see is to believe. There really is damage being done to the brain whenever an addiction takes hold. Once one sees the damage that addiction can bring to the brain, it can boost motivation to successfully live the lives God intended.

The "physiology of addiction" is:

> the body's ability to adjust to the substance by incorporating the substance into its 'normal' functioning. This state creates the conditions of tolerance and withdrawal. Tolerance is the process by which the body continually adapts to the substance and requires increasingly larger amounts to achieve the original effects. Withdrawal refers to physical and psychological symptoms experienced when reducing or discontinuing a substance that the body has

become dependent on. Symptoms of withdrawal generally include but are not limited to anxiety, irritability, intense cravings for the substance, nausea, hallucinations, headaches, cold sweats, and tremors.[5]

The ability to see the effects on the brain throughout the addiction process helps us respect it as a holy temple. The increase and decrease of brain chemicals during physiological dependence, tolerance, and withdrawal helps us understand the behavioral dynamics of bad habits and addictions.

Scientists are developing new understandings about many human problems and noting how the choices we make affect the brain's physical structure (anatomy) and functional organization (physiology) including the neural pathways and synapses developed (often termed the brain's neuroplasticity). Research on brain imaging is beginning to show how certain thoughts and behavior, or the environment, or injury, can change neural processes.

In the 2011 Dawn Farm Education Series, Carl Christensen, explored "the differences in neurochemistry between the addicted brain and the normal brain, the progression of physiological changes that occur in chemically dependent individuals, the mechanisms of physiologic tolerance and withdrawal, and the effects of

---

[5] Torres G, Horowitz JM (1999). "Drugs of abuse and brain gene expression". *Psychosom Med.* **61** (5): 630–50.

treatment on the addicted brain."[6] He points out that the brain imaging of blood flow and dopamine underscore what addicts and counselors have long understood about the craving, compulsion, and loss of control despite awareness of the consequences of use. That is:

- Addiction causes damage to the neurotransmitter system in the brain which makes the individual feel depleted because their primary chemical transmitter, dopamine, which provides pleasure and rewards, is not firing properly.

- To get the same feeling of well-being or normal satisfactions in life, much more of the addiction substance or behavior is required but this only causes greater damage and a stronger impulse in the future.

- The long-term damage is real, the brain images of two 43-year-old men, one addict, the other not, is strikingly different, with the addict's brain being significantly smaller, and blank spaces within the brain are larger.

Over forty years ago, it used to be said by educators that brain cells are destroyed when we drink alcohol. The words can no longer fall on deaf ears, as we now know this is true. Christensen also notes that brain images display the fact that the natural repair of the biological

---

[6] Carl Christensen, Wayne State University School of Medicine, Dawn Farm Education Series, 2011.

system of the brain takes much longer than typically expected. For example, while most formal treatment detoxification periods are from ten days to one month, the brain imaging studies show that the brain is not able to repair itself even in 90 days and is not more fully functioning until after about a one and one-half year period of complete abstinence.[7]

Excerpts from the July 2004 issue of the Harvard Mental Health Letter, entitled, "The Addicted Brain" further describe the biological mechanisms underlying the addiction process:

> When a human being or other animal performs an action that satisfies a need or fulfills a desire, the neurotransmitter dopamine is released into the nucleus accumbens and produces pleasure. It serves as a signal that the action promotes survival or reproduction, directly or indirectly. The system is called the reward pathway. When we do something that provides this reward, the brain records the experience and we are likely to do it again. Damage to the nucleus accumbens and drugs that block dopamine release in the region make everything less rewarding. In nature, rewards usually come only with effort and after a delay. Addictive drugs provide a shortcut.

---

[7] Ibid.

Each in its own way sets in motion a biological process that results in flooding the nucleus accumbens with dopamine. The pleasure is not serving survival or reproduction, and evolution has not provided our brains with an easy way to withstand the onslaught. In a person who becomes addicted through repeated use of a drug, overwhelmed receptor cells call for a shutdown. The natural capacity to produce dopamine in the reward system is reduced, while the need persists and the drug seems to be the only way to fulfill it. The brain is losing its access to other, less immediate and powerful sources of reward. Addicts may require constantly higher doses and a quicker passage into the brain. It's as though the normal machinery of motivation is no longer functioning; they want the drug even when it no longer gives pleasure. Addictive drugs provide a shortcut to the brain's reward system by flooding the nucleus accumbens with dopamine. The hippocampus lays down memories of this rapid sense of satisfaction, and the amygdala creates a conditioned response to certain stimuli. [8]

The "relapse mechanism" demonstrates the physiological "bondage of the brain" described in detail as follows:

---

[8] Monthly issue of the Harvard Mental Health Letter, "The Addicted Brain. July 2004.

Changes in the reward system alone cannot explain why addiction persists. As Mark Twain said of his tobacco habit, quitting is easy; he had done it often. Many addicts go through long periods without taking the drug, but they risk relapse even after years of abstinence, when the dopamine reward circuit has had plenty of time to recuperate. They are victims of conditioned learning, which creates habitual responses.

Drug-induced changes in the links between brain cells establish associations between the drug experience and the circumstances in which it occurred. These implicit memories can be retrieved when addicts are exposed to any reminder of those circumstances — moods, situations, people, places, or the substance itself. A heroin addict may be in danger of relapse when she sees a hypodermic needle, an alcoholic when he passes a bar where he used to drink or when he meets a former drinking companion. Any addict may resume the habit on falling into a mood in which he used to turn to the drug. A single small dose of the drug itself is one of the most powerful reminders — "It's the first drink that gets you drunk," as they say in Alcoholics Anonymous.

Internal or external stress is another cause of relapse. The nucleus accumbens sends signals to the amygdala and hippocampus, which register and consolidate memories that evoke strong feelings. When asked why they relapse, addicts may say, "My job was not going well," or even, "The traffic was so heavy that day." These answers suggest that they are hypersensitive to stress, either congenitally or as a result of past addiction. Levels of corticotropin releasing hormone (CRH), the brain chemical that regulates the stress hormone system, often rise in addicts just before a relapse, while the amygdala becomes more active. Mice bred without receptors for CRH are less susceptible to drug addiction.[9]

Excerpts *From the Voice*, (a Hazelden publication, a national provider of addiction treatment services), in a 2001 article entitled "Addiction: A brain disease with biological underpinnings" provide additional insights:

In a recent article, Alan Leshner, PhD, director of the National Institute on Drug Abuse, claims that "Every drug user starts out as an occasional user, and that initial use is a voluntary and controllable decision, but as time passes and drug use continues, a person goes from being a voluntary to a compulsive drug user. This change occurs because over time, use of addictive drugs changes the brain--at times in big dramatic toxic ways, at others in more subtle ways, but always

---

[9] Ibid.

in destructive ways that can result in compulsive and even uncontrollable drug use."

Autopsies consistently show that chronic alcoholics have lighter and smaller brains than other people of the same age and gender. Researchers have also observed this shrinking effect in living alcoholics through non-invasive medical tests that give a picture of the brain in action. These tests include magnetic resonance imaging (MRI), positron emission tomography (PET) scans, and computed tomography (CT) scans. According to the National Institute on Alcohol Abuse and Alcoholism, alcoholic dementia is the second-leading cause of adult dementia in the United States, exceeded only by Alzheimers disease. Addictive drugs wreak havoc with the normal exchange of neurotransmitters in countless ways.[10]

Understanding the many chemical processes in the brain is a prerequisite toward explaining the habit-forming nature of certain substances. This knowledge can be used to help the Youth especially, avoid the chemical craving that entraps them early on.

---

[10] Excerpts *From the Voice*, Hazelden publications: "Addiction: A brain disease with biological underpinnings." 2001.

Chapter 3

Treating Dependency

Determining "dependence" on drugs/alcohol is widely debated and there is no complete agreement as to when a person exhibiting bad habits is "addicted." Yet with each addiction to substance, impulsive control disorder, and obsessive-compulsive behavior, there is one common theme. The commonality is that a person truly loses track of their God-centered self. In being overwhelmed with the demands of complying with the addiction, there is often a complete failure to see the source of the problem.

It is very easy to succumb to an addiction, though not always as easy to stop it in its tracks. Usually, it only takes some sensitivity of the control it has on us, and this awareness is enough to cause one to stop it by abstaining from the behavior altogether. Sometimes however, the physiological, psychological, and behavioral pull makes breaking the addiction very difficult, and the longer it endures, the more difficult it is to get rid of and more problematic it becomes.

Professionals tasked with treating addiction have had a difficult time as there is no simple pill that will take care of the problem. The *Harvard Letter* notes:

> The more scientists learn about addiction, the clearer it becomes that chemical solutions will

not be available soon. For the foreseeable future, medications will be only an aid to psychosocial treatment. We will still need 12-step self-help groups, behavioral therapies, and exploration of traumatic and everyday experiences that may have disturbed the balance of the reward and inhibition system or the process of learning by association.

Behavior therapy provides sources of reward and punishment that compete with the drug, such as payment for clean urine in the form of vouchers, or contingency contracts (in which addicts agree to give up something important to them if they go back to using the drug). Behavior therapists also work to change the learned associations that create the risk of relapse.

Motivation or will can be regarded as a brain function that is damaged by addiction, just as language or movement can be damaged by a stroke. In successful treatment of a stroke, other parts of the brain assume the functions of the injured region. In the same way, treatment for addiction may be able to make use of the remaining healthy parts of the motivation system to repair the damage. Twelve-step groups and motivational enhancement therapy could be seen as ways of accomplishing that.

Treatment will always depend on the type of addiction and the type of addict. Novelty seekers and risk takers with insufficient inhibition and judgment will not necessarily respond to the same methods that work for people afflicted by traumatic stress or hypersensitivity to everyday stress. And the most important lesson of all in recent discoveries may be that addictions are chronic conditions for which there are treatments but rarely simple cures.

The new brain research suggests that addiction is not just a property of certain drugs but an aspect of certain human activities and relationships. Researchers have already found resemblances between the brain scan images of compulsive gamblers and drug addicts. The idea of addiction to television, video games, overeating, or sexual behavior may be more than a metaphor. Exploring the biology of addiction could lead to a deeper understanding of the sources of all human motivation and habit formation.[11]

Turning to God

Through brain imaging scientists can now see the differences between healthy and unhealthy brains and connect that to substance abuse and obsessive problem behaviors. Education to the public on research on animal models and functional brain imaging on humans can be helpful in demonstrating the chemical and neurotransmitter changes associated with addiction. This

---

[11] Ibid, *The Harvard Letter*.

can be a useful tool for motivating individuals toward corrective actions of all sorts of problem behaviors.

While it is important to see brain imaging, to understand the physiological damage being done and see why there is the psychological compulsion toward addictive behaviors, it typically still takes discipline and a deep determination to break the habit of addiction. That is why the 12 Step Program relies on God's help to bring calm to the storm and order to the chaos in one's life.

The following are the original twelve steps as published by Alcoholics Anonymous:[12]

1. We admitted we were powerless over alcohol— that our lives had become unmanageable.
2. Came to believe that a Power greater than ourselves could restore us to sanity.
3. Made a decision to turn our will and our lives over to the care of **God** *as we understood Him*.
4. Made a searching and fearless moral inventory of ourselves.
5. Admitted to God, to ourselves, and to another human being the exact nature of our wrongs.
6. Were entirely ready to have God remove all these defects of character.
7. Humbly asked Him to remove our shortcomings.
8. Made a list of all persons we had harmed, and became willing to make amends to them all.

---

[12] Bill W., *Alcoholics Anonymous* (4th ed.). Alcoholics Anonymous World Services. June 2001.

9. Made direct amends to such people wherever possible, except when to do so would injure them or others.
10. Continued to take personal inventory, and when we were wrong, promptly admitted it.
11. Sought **through prayer and meditation to** improve our conscious contact with God *as we understood Him*, praying only for knowledge of His will for us and the power to carry that out.
12. Having had a spiritual awakening as the result of these steps, we tried to carry this message to alcoholics, and to practice these principles in all our affairs.

The twelve-step program helps provide a social structure to strengthen resolve and commitment to change. We come to understand our dependence upon God to help overcome the destructive forces of worldly attachment that only confuse, frustrate, and cause the lack of need fulfillment. These principles within the Twelve Step process reflect the core messages of Jesus. An examination of conscience and a firm commitment to change and give up any evil tendencies is critical to any constructive change and improvement of self. There is no better time than the present to correct one's attitudes, beliefs, and actions to meet true needs.

In his inauguration Mass, Pope Benedict reminded us of the same words spoken so often by his predecessor, Pope John Paul II, who at his own inauguration cited the words so frequently spoken by Christ: "Do not be afraid." To this, Pope Benedict added:

"Do not be afraid of Christ! He takes nothing away, and He gives you everything. When we give ourselves to Him, we receive a hundredfold in return. Yes, open, open wide the doors to Christ—and you will find true life."[13]

Do not be afraid to build on the improvement. That is, once the reconstruction project has begun, the renovation process can really be quite fantastic. It's not just about sustaining one's energy, meeting the difficult task at hand, overcoming an addiction and making a comeback, it is about living in the joy of the Spirit and becoming better than ever…in fact, being the best one can be and maybe even being better than one could ever have been.

Some strategies that can help to build on improvement are to:

- Adapt a Corrective Action Plan;
- Develop a Faith Journal;
- Focus on a Balanced Approach; and
- Strive for Integration.

Incorporate the Corrective Action Plan. Use the corrective action plan and narrative (to be described in the next chapter) to keep corrective actions on course. Periodically review the twelve-step process and focus attention on problem spots. There is no making peace with the devil. There is no middle ground or compromise.

---

[13] Pope Benedict XVI, Words from his inauguration Mass.

One cannot serve God and others, and the Devil at the same time. Remember, our thoughts and actions have consequences. There is no such thing as a victimless crime. Choosing God will bring rewards richer than one can imagine; choosing evil brings sure failure and punishment, eventually.

Develop a Faith Journal. It is said that every step we take toward God, however little, is a bold leap into the loving arms of our Savior. And so, we look carefully in an introspective manner to uncover potential blind spots or areas that improvements are needed. To help with this process, one needs to keep track of daily habits, attitudes and actions, and strive to appreciate God's graces more and live life fully. A "faith journal" will help to document one's journey, thoughts and revelations, experiences and challenges, prayers and insights.

Focus on a Balanced Approach. Personal balance requires a continuous feeding of the four interrelated areas of personal well-being: the mind, body, soul, and social/emotional dimensions of the heart. Each area is vital to develop because when problems develop in any one part of the whole, the whole is affected. Bodily illness affects the mind; mental problems stress the body; charitable acts improve one's heart and spirit. Relatively simple practices of nurturing each area daily can eliminate complex, costly and time-consuming problems from developing. Being "well-rounded" means striving to develop all four parts of one's being without ignoring any. Track the activity and time spent improving in each area as part of one's daily journal and see how one's overall well-being is improved.

Strive for Integration. Another strategy for improving oneself is borrowed from Zen psychology and can be called the integration of the whole being. The critical processes of integration are to:

- Focus attention confidently on a key aspect of the present most critical to success;

- See without judging;

- Develop a clear image of goal behavior;

- Relax and perform effortlessly; and,

- Trust and respond naturally.

By using the principles of integration, one reduces the concern for self-evaluation and the dependence upon external indicators of success. By not being so self-conscience about things that are unimportant, one is free to improve without impediments imposed by the mind and the perceptions felt from others' judgment.

The integration principle will be covered later, but in short, it provides the freedom needed for improvement, so that instead of exerting great effort to achieve change, we are able to let go and allow it to happen naturally. The integration principles are used to increase trust, relaxation, and awareness, and to minimize personally destructive judgments and strivings, so to disengage one's own unnecessary subjective concerns.

Thus, to find a spiritual focus when serving the needy, one tries to see "the image of Jesus" in the homeless man, the sick, the mentally ill, the elderly, the abused child, the victim, the troubled, the sinner, the imprisoned, or the lonely person. One might also look for "the innocent child" within others, and there one can see the spirit of God in all people, rich or poor, healthy or sick, young or old.

When praying, one wants to talk to God and listen to Him, as if there is no distance or delay in the discussion, because there isn't. Focus on the words as being the voice of God when reading the Bible, singing religious hymns, or listening to sermons. Also, take time when engaging with God and speak softly a prayer as if speaking directly to God, because indeed, you are. Repeat the words of scripture softly to oneself when they are being read by another. These things enhance concentration and memory, and the experience of the spirit is magnified the more one focuses and engages the senses.

Keep the Ultimate Goal Clear

Today's culture shuns the improvement of spirituality and moral or religious knowledge because it is steeped in relativism, which is driven by selfish motives. It is a truism that: "The wise man desires what he needs; the fool desires what he wants. When we cannot learn to govern ourselves, we will surely be governed by fools."

This applies to the fool within and the fools outside of us who seek to misguide. In seeking the goal, meeting one's true needs, we strive to willingly and freely live by God's rules and by His Greatest Commandment. Living by God's rules is reflected in both how we think and what we say. A priest once said: "when we speak, be sure to say only what is true, necessary, and edifying." "Edifying" does not mean to say what is pleasing to another or may be politically correct, it means to say what is "instructive toward the improvement of spirituality; what establishes or builds a moral or religious knowledge."[14]

Once one comes to surrender their life to God, one is no longer like a car spinning its wheels on ice, but rather like one who finds traction and life moves forward with new purpose, God's purpose. In trusting in God, the more one stays focused on doing the little things right, the more grace begins to come into one's life and the more wonderful life becomes.

Developing faith in, hope for, and love of, God and neighbor as self, is like the process of arranging a complex puzzle. At first, one slowing and awkwardly tries to fit the pieces together…that is, matching thoughts and actions with what one knows God would want. Then the picture slowly starts to come together…and after a while one can make a little more sense of what God wants. Finally, with more effort in doing the next right and loving thing, one starts to see the whole puzzle picture coming

---

[14] Webster's dictionary.

together…and proceeds with much greater ease as one begins to see the beauty of the big picture. The constant living by His command and rising to meet His unique plan for one's life is the path to freedom through virtue. It is certainly worth the time and effort.

The physical, mental, social development of an individual are all connected to make us who we are. When any problem develops in the brain, we must search for the origin or cause. Has there been some history of abuse of the body, mind, or soul of the individual? Was there anything severe that occurred recently to impact the individual, a sudden loss of a family member or best friend, a sudden realization about oneself or pending in one's future? Has anything of a serious nature or traumatic event been repressed from early childhood or adolescence?

The effort to find the cause of the mental problem is perhaps the single most important issue for overcoming the problem. When finding a cause and an immediate relief through counseling is not enough, then finding the right medicine is necessary to provide the chemical balance necessary to stabilize the individual's physiology. Finally, it is important to create an environment where the patient, as well as one's family and friends, all understand and become educated on the physiological challenge to overcome the mental and behavior difficulties, and how everyone plays a role in helping the individual and themselves.

Turning to God is the answer to much of the "conflict, confusion, fear, and bad habits" that perpetuate the self-destructive cycle.   The General Human Condition presents a challenge to each person attempting to meet their needs. Today's therapists certainly have a challenge in responding to psychoses, phobias and addictions, and should be advised to not forget that prayer, repentance, forgiveness, and the grace of God are there to lend help.

The continuing development of drugs and chemicals to support the efforts of those in the fields of psychology, social psychology, and psychiatry have enhanced the treatment of mental illness. In the process, however, we must not lose sight of Who made us and what we are made of. The endeavor to overcome behavioral problems and mental illnesses should not ignore or forget the One that created the brain and Who sustains us all. The secret weapon of the best professionals is still turning to the source, The Creator, who gave the gift of the brain, to help resolve even the most difficult problems.

Chapter 4

Getting Better

One company that has become very successful in moving packages, "Federal Express," has a very simple motto. "If it can be tracked, it will be improved." This company tracks every step of its shipping process and assures packages get delivered on time. They have used the simple art of tracking and accounting for the time at every phase of its operation to continuously improve itself, making it the industry leader.

Their success has implications to almost anything that needs improvement, including self-improvement and even the ability to meet true needs. Becoming aware of the need for improvement is the start of the process. And the first step toward constructive change is the commitment to track progress.

Strategies for Improving

The ability to meet life's challenges and to assess and correct one's attitudes and behavior requires an honest accounting of one's thoughts and behaviors. In his epistle to the Galatians, St. Paul reminds us how we are to live, urging us to "Walk in the Spirit, and you will not fulfill the desires of the flesh." (Galatians 5:16) He warns against "immorality" and sin of all kind, and that:

"They who do such things will not attain the kingdom of God. But the fruit of the Spirit is: charity, joy, peace, patience, kindness, goodness, faith, modesty, and continency" (self-restraint from yielding to impulse or desire) (Galatians 5:22-23).

The result of meeting true needs is attaining the fruits of the Spirit, but before this can occur, we must do our part, that is, take responsibility and be self-disciplined. This includes doing our best to "meet God halfway." If we put in the effort and do our part; God will do the rest.

Any strategy for self-improvement involves "assessing, correcting, and tracking." This includes knowing where we are, seeing where we want to go and going there, by keeping ourselves on course. Adjustments and improvements are continuous. Like Federal Express, the tracking of progress provides accountability and helps determine the degree to which goals were achieved, what conditions helped or hindered accomplishment, if goals were reasonable or appropriate, and if better processes and methods can be implemented to improve results.

Some useful concepts and strategies for self-improvement that are aided by tracking include:

- self-awareness;
- self-control;
- self-worth; and
- situational awareness.

Self-Awareness

The meeting of true needs begins with self-awareness and honesty. For example, we need to be loved as well as need to love others; need to be respected and valued by others, as well as respect and value others. Part of the fulfillment of needs then is often dependent upon one's truthful appraisal of oneself and other's perceptions. A very useful analytical tool for objectively examining and tracking the perceptions of self and others' is using the Johari window.[15]

The following displays the congruence or non-congruence of one's self-perceptions with the perceptions of others, about oneself and others.

The Johari Window

Things about self that others:	*Things about self that I:* Do Know	Do Not know
Do Know	Common knowledge	Blind spots
Do Not Know	Secrets	Unknown self

The four outcomes of the Johari Window then are:

Common knowledge gained by sharing oneself with

---

[15] J. Luft, "The Johari Window," Human Relations and Training News, Jan 1961, p 6-7.

others and by requesting and receiving honest feedback from others. The more the effort to share in this way, the greater is the area of common knowledge and the more likely is the fulfillment of needs.

Unknown Self where an individual is unwilling to see their faults clearly yet is able to hide them from others.

Blind Spots are the result of individuals being too unwitting or insensitive to accept others' verbal or non-verbal criticism.

Secrets are the result of one trying to maintain one's privacy, but it is often at the expense of sharing more deeply of oneself with someone special.

Johari contends that there is matching as well as incongruent perceptions between one's self-insight and the perspective of others about oneself. This dynamic produces four distinct states of self-understanding. Congruent perceptions, the healthiest option for sustaining mutual relationships, are gained by sharing oneself with others and by requesting and receiving honest feedback from others ("common knowledge"). The remaining three possibilities often tend to cause stress and problems. That is, the "unknown self," "blind spots," and "secrets" lead to confusion, insensitivity toward others, and personal misconceptions that make the meeting of needs more difficult. To make improvements in these categories, track self-awareness and see how your relationships strengthen as perception of self and others grow.

Common knowledge is almost a prerequisite for the fulfillment of needs of mutual respect and love, and indeed, many of our social problems can be overcome through our congruence of understanding. In seeking that, it is essential to treat others with the same dignity and respect we might wish for ourselves. It is critical here to not pre-judge others nor hastily judge others by the externalities of physical appearance. Also, holding on to secrets fails to enable us to know whether others might relate to us and begin to form a deeper bond so we might know them. Fear that self-disclosure will result in possible rejection and betrayal of trust and privacy is a real concern, but without such effort, the rewards of common knowledge and understanding are sacrificed.

Self-Control

Critical to changing one's behavior is tracking it and holding oneself accountable for doing the right thing. Tracking improvement in self-control is important for maintaining mastery over one's own life. Keeping a personal tracking guide can help improve the awareness of problems, monitor the corrective actions taken and overcome personal problems. The basic concepts of the self-control model involve the identification of:

> ***A. Negative Outside Influences***: the conditions of one's environment or social relations that promote the development of self-control problems.

B. *Inherent Weaknesses*: refers to the types of personal susceptibilities one is inclined toward having and the problems that result. (One with a personal weakness to alcohol, for example, is at high risk when entering a bar.)

C. *Safeguards*: all efforts, abilities and mechanisms used to overcome negative outside influences and inherent weaknesses. The idea is to put safeguards into place to prevent internal control problems. (A self-assessment of A and B above, and the identification of C, is the foundation for a plan of action which is then tested and tracked for success within specific time periods.)

Self-Control Rating: is a general measure of the level of self-control (high, medium, low), based on one's self-assessment of the previous three areas. (For example, if there are negative outside influences for a person with high inherent weakness to them, and there are ineffective safeguards in place, then the risk of problems is high, and the self-control rating is low. Likewise, if there are few negative outside influences and little inherent weakness and adequate safeguards in place just in case, then one's risk for problems is low and their self-control rating is high).

Corrective Actions Need to Be Taken: this is needed whenever there are low or medium self-control ratings. A corrective action plan should be developed that will reduce or eliminate negative outside influences or internal weaknesses by making improvements through stronger safeguards. The idea is to lower risk of problems and increase self-control.

Tracking Results of Actions: actual results and outcomes of processes need to be monitored and documented to make continuous improvements. The tracking and self-evaluation demonstrates the effectiveness of the corrective actions taken. If the actions were ineffective, a new plan is needed. If the actions were effective, the safeguards just need to be maintained.

Thus, after an assessment of one's negative outside influences and inherent weaknesses, a selection of safeguards is identified to prevent the occurrence of problems. Then a plan of action is developed (corrective action plan) designed to improve and control behavior. Improving behavior and self-control does not mean sacrificing freedom. On the contrary, it is the most powerful vehicle for asserting one's own rights and protecting the individual rights of others.

Whenever people follow their own compulsive desires (or those of others), they are no longer free and independent but rather are a slave to their own or other's disorientations. Indeed, only when actions are controlled do we have peace of mind, the ability to freely learn and create, have a sense of humor, and are able to engage in meaningful interaction and human relations.

When one does not have a healthy sense of internal control, their present and future state of existence becomes uncertain. An internal control plan should keep the big picture of meeting true needs clearly in mind and begin with a prayer to God for help to overcome one's own weaknesses, troubling behavior, and selfishness that causes problems. Individuals are more prone to problems when they feel confused, lost to one's true self. This state of confusion leads to problems as emotions range from being uncertain to being concerned and worried, to being fearful and afraid. A personal journal can be used to describe the issues, feelings, and results from the internal control implementation. This narrative account will support the tracking and evaluation process, and help diminish backsliding or getting side tracked, distracted, or off course.

Self-Worth

More than any previous generation, today's children are pressed into a daily series of non-stop activities all their waking moments in a constant pursuit of being the best they can be (or sadly what their parents wish them to be as they often seem to live their lives vicariously through them). Often lost in the hurry to accomplish the most in school, sports, and cultural activities, however, is the meeting of true needs.

Since our value and worth has a divine imprint, our future is limited only when we fail to see the nature of our existence and the nature of our relationship to God, our Creator. Our relations with others are limited only when we fail to see that the same God made all human beings and that each person is highly treasured in His eyes, with a distinct purpose to serve Him.

Regina Brett was a 90-year-old commentator with the Cleveland Plain Dealer newspaper, when she shared with her readers some pithy words of wisdom from lessons she learned over the years. Her epigrams put things quite well in perspective and include the following:

- God loves you because of who God is, not because of anything you did or didn't do.

- Forgive everyone everything.

- What other people think of you is none of your business.

- Time heals almost everything. Give time, time.

- However good or bad a situation is, it will change.

- Don't take yourself so seriously. No one else does.

- All that really matters in the end is that you truly loved.

- Get outside every day. Miracles are waiting everywhere.

- Life isn't tied with a bow, but it's still a gift.

Our self-worth must be tied to the true image of who we come from. The clearer that image, the more secure we will be.

God tells us to love, and we do because we know He loves us. He tells us to forgive as part of that love and we do because we know He does. God makes every situation good in some way, but we may need time to understand it and will need to keep our eyes on Him to see it. If we trust in Him through our changing situation and keep a humble view of ourselves, we will find Him there. Strive to always see God in others, for it is people not things that ultimately matter in this world, and above all, love matters most. Documenting personal observations and insights about self-worth in a journal over time will enrich one's understanding on the value of life itself and keep one's true needs in focus.

Situational-Awareness

People generally fall into a pattern as to how they respond to situations, and that difference makes all the difference in outcomes. Alberti and Emmons[16] have shown there is a significant difference in outcome

---

[16] R.E. Alberti and M.L. Emmons, *Your Perfect Right*, San Lius Obispo, CA: Impact.

between those responding to stressful situations appropriately with assertive behavior, as opposed to those responding inappropriately with aggressive behavior or diversionary behavior (fight/flight reaction).

Tracking one's response to all types of stressful situations improves awareness and helps correct behaviors that need to become more assertive and appropriate. Responding appropriately to stress can be seen in the following simple examples of work, family and social situations, where aggressive behavior and diversionary behaviors are shown as clear contrasts to a more "situation appropriate" assertive responses.

Work: Personal Performance Evaluation

Situation: Mark receives his personnel performance rating given by his manager and is disappointed by several low ratings.

Aggressive: After a brief analysis of the manager's written explanation of the ratings, Mark storms into the manager's office and demands that the ratings be changed. The boss becomes further alienated and adamant about the ratings.

Diversionary: Mark is upset by the low scores and turns to others to vent, whine and whimper; and at every opportunity, criticizes his boss. Otherwise, he does nothing to understand, address the issue, or correct the perceived problems.

Situation Appropriate: Mark makes an appointment to meet with the manager. He brings evidence of work or other support information to his bolster case. Mark pinpoints ratings that he believes should be higher and presents facts and opinions on the matter. Boss seriously reconsiders ratings, responds with clearer feedback, and Mark accepts the suggestions and promises to take corrective actions.

Work: Managing People - the Team Leader

Situation: Kevin is a team leader of a major research project supervising three individuals. Two individuals are contributing well to the accomplishment of the project; one individual, Peter, is not doing his best.

Aggressive: Kevin berates Peter before his peers, tells him his work is totally inadequate, and then reports on the matter to his supervisor and requests that Peter be replaced on the project.

Diversionary: Kevin ignores the problem with Peter's work and compensates by doing Peter's work for him.

Situation Appropriate: Kevin discusses the issue of Peter's work in private with him providing specific examples of the problem. Kevin then asks, "What can be done about it?" Together Kevin and Peter develop a mutually agreeable solution to the dilemma, setting specific goals and procedures for monitoring future progress.

Social: Meeting People

Situation: Mike is 24 and works in construction. All his co-workers participate in girl watching and calling out to every attractive female that passes by. One particular girl, Elsie, that Mike is interested in, likes to eat at a nearby restaurant.

Aggressive: Mike becomes active if not king of the cat-callers. He becomes louder and most obvious when Elsie walks by. One day he walks over, stands in her path, and asks for a date. Elsie says no and walks away and avoids that path in the future.

Diversionary: Mike mildly participates in the cat-calling but accepts the notion that he will never meet Elsie.

Situation Appropriate: Mike does not participate in the cat-calling and tries to correct those who do. He then takes a day off work, goes to the restaurant where Elsie works and at an appropriate and opportune time, introduces himself to her. They talk for a few seconds and Mike asks her if she would like to have company for lunch. She is pleased and while together at lunch, Mike tells Elsie how he has seen her on her daily walks to work and advises she consider another route to avoid his co-workers' cat-calls. He apologizes for them. He also asks her for a date on the weekend. She accepts.

Social: Peer Pressure – Just saying "No"

Situation: Mike is a high school senior. The crowd he hangs around with drinks regularly and has begun exploring drug usage. Mike has resisted all along but receives increasing pressure from his buddies who of course are very important to him. It has reached a point where Mike is the only one in his crowd to refuse to drink alcohol or do drugs. The pressure is enormous because there is nothing for Mike to do while the others consume the alcohol and/or drugs. Mike becomes more of an "outcast" once his friends are under the influence, and he can no longer relate to their behavior and at the same time their ridiculing of his resistance becomes more offensive.

Aggressive: Mike decides he can no longer take the abuse. The next time anyone makes an offensive remark he plans to reel off a few knockout punches.

Diversionary: Mike decides to give in and try whatever alcohol and drugs his friends have just to maintain or enhance his relationship with the group. He decides to compromise by just having smaller portions of everything so not to get out-of-control, because he really doesn't want anything. (He does not think he will become hooked or have any problem with this low-key approach. He could be mistaken.)

Situation Appropriate: Mike notices that the group only consumes alcohol and drugs on the weekends, and particularly when preparing for a party, dance or concert. Mike encourages his friends to stop doing drugs and vastly reduce the amount of alcohol; and for safety purposes to set up one person to drive who has no alcohol/drug consumption. Mike agrees to be the first driver but wants everyone to take his or her turn at driving while abstaining from drinking and drugs for the night along with him. If this method is rejected or unsuccessful, Mike plans to find other friends to spend the weekend nights with and keeps a firm stance against drinking and drugs.

In any number or variety of life situations, stresses, and fears, it is important to find the appropriate response. This is almost always the assertive response, as opposed to aggression or diversion, which often leads to destructive results toward others or oneself.

The prolonged neglect and inability to self-correct misbehavior creates even more stress and problems. When one does not deal effectively with the existing stress and life situations, it only adds more strain to their life. In contrast, the more in tune one is with true needs, the greater will be self-awareness, self-control, self-worth, and appropriate response to life issues, problems, and situations.

Chapter 5

Firm Resolve to Attain Goals

Clear mental awareness of the objective, accountability to a specific action plan, and a strong desire to fulfill one's true purpose is vital to maintaining the resolve necessary for the effective meeting of goals, including meeting one's true needs. Resolution comes from a spark of inspiration and from a firestorm of determination.

Procrastination and distraction are the destructive intervening variables that often arise when moving from inspiration to determination. When Moses went up Mount Sinai to meet with God, the Israelites became bored and disgruntled, lost their resolve to wait patiently in obedience and turned to idolatry. Idleness is the devil's workshop and during such times, temptations can intervene and threaten to destroy resolve and knock one off course.

To find and maintain strong resolve:

- Develop a clear image of the behavior to be achieved.

- Implement that behavior as flawlessly as possible for a considerable number of days (such as a full month).

- Do not allow past mistakes and failures to cause new mistakes or failures. Learn from the past, rather than "giving in" to the present because of failures of the past. Each day is a new day and the chance for a better way.

- Produce a mental image of fulfilling objectives even under adverse conditions. Do not let self-doubt and fear of the unknown get in the way. Be creative and make necessary adjustments if need be to stay on course.

- Be actively, rather than passively, resistant to all temptations, even the littlest tests of your will.

Realize that by resisting the devil's temptations, one pleases God. In fighting against idleness, procrastination, distractions, deceptions, and diversions, one is battling some of the best punches the devil can bring.

Know When to Seek Help

Before one's life or that of a loved one is entangled in a destructive "problem cycle" spiraling downward with problems getting bigger and more out of control, one needs to seek outside help. Try to find a spiritual minister, counselor, psychologist, or psychiatrist before the problem becomes so entrenched and hardened, that it appears hopeless.

Only a physician or psychiatrist can prescribe

medicine to provide a better chemical balance in the brain or recommend a chemical desensitization treatment. If the problem has become too great for the individual to change by themselves, one of the most effective change strategies, as mentioned before, is the 12 Step program developed by Alcoholics Anonymous.[17] While it may not be effective in all cases, it has helped many, and multitudes of addicts that have tried every available alternative confess it is the only thing that works.

The 12 Step program brings addicted individuals together into a group loyal toward helping one another through the steps of change needed to become responsible and productive citizens again. It is designed so that each member shares something about their own experience and receives insight from others with similar experiences. The group experience breaks down barriers of rationalizations, excuses, and other resistance. As a result, no longer does one feel alone in the journey toward stability and improved control over one's situation. It is one of the most effective ways to help someone get back on the right track and stay on track.

The 12 Step program is really a personal pact with God to work and trust in Him, to allow God to take control over the compulsive disorder and to free one of the strains of such problems. The 12 Step program has been so successful that there is now such a program to address the concerns of almost every form of troubling human

---

[17] AA World Services. *Alcoholics Anonymous*. NY: Alcoholics Anonymous World Services, 1939.

problems and addictions, with programs for the addicted
as well as for their families affected by the illness.

All 12 Step programs follow the same rules for
recovery. These programs can be grouped according to
the major type of issues addressed or broad cause of
addiction. Although there may be overlapping causes,
some of the primary addiction programs are:

Issues with Substance Abuse:

> **Alcoholics Anonymous**--for those who wish to
> stop drinking. (Al-Anon-for those affected by
> another's drinking. Alates-for teenagers and Al-
> Atots-for children affected by parents drinking.
> Adult Children of Alcoholics-for adults whose
> parents were or are alcoholics.)

> **Narcotics Anonymous**--for people addicted to
> drugs. (Nar-Anon-for people affected by another
> person's drug addiction.)

> **Overeaters Anonymous**--for people with eating
> disorders. (O-Anon--for people affected by
> someone's' eating problems.)

Issues with Responsibilities and Emotions:

> **Parents Anonymous**--for parents who are
> abusive or neglectful of their responsibilities.

> **Families Anonymous**--for people concerned

about any type of compulsive or behavior problem of a relative or friend.

Emotions Anonymous--for people who desire to become well emotionally.

Issues with Money, Power, Pleasure:

Gamblers Anonymous--for people who desire to stop their compulsive gambling. (Gam-Anon-for individuals affected by others' gambling.)

Sex Addicts Anonymous--for individuals with compulsive sexual addiction. (Co-SA-for others affected by those with sexual addiction.)

The devil works and plays with souls by driving them to self-destruction as they seek relief from their conflicts, confusion, fears, stresses and challenges. The 12 Step Program requires everyone to turn to God and call on Him for strength. It is both an acknowledgement of God and wholesale rejection of the devil, and a realization that ignoring and denying God in the past is what has led to most people's downfall.

The primary underlying cause for the perpetuation of such uncontrollable problems is the inability to resist the evil spirit. Accounting for it to others and getting clear insights from others with similar problems is the way to develop a strong understanding about the nature of the problem, and a firm will to work through the issues and challenges to meet the problems head-on.

All addictions are primarily caused by the deadly desires for money, power, pleasure, and esteem, provoked by the cardinal sins of gluttony, pride, wrath, lust, envy, greed and sloth. The 12 steps toward overcoming any addiction do not consist of some mystical mix of ingredients, they are simply a fundamental set of Christian principles that lead one to develop a personal relationship with God, and an accountability for one's actions to others and oneself. This is the essence toward getting back in touch with our true needs, to fulfill the Greatest Commandment. (The 12 Step Program reflect the essential process undertaken by any Catholic during the Sacrament of Penance or Reconciliation and is the inspiration for the program from the start.)

The Twelve Step programs are non-promotional non-profit groups, free and open to anyone who wants to attend. The programs are designed to address special problems by bringing people together with common problems in a respectful manner to listen and help each other. The format of the meetings varies somewhat but the purpose is for each member of the group to be able to progress in development through the 12 steps over as many meetings as is needed, participating at one's own emotional pace.

The discussion of personal failings and personal experiences are offset by the positive examples of others overcoming similar difficulties and describing the healing process. The meetings provide peer support and encouragement and are a living testament of God's redeeming presence and enduring love among those striving to meet their true needs.

Planning and Implementation of Improvements

Decide on a long-term vision. Start with the desirable end results and work backwards when developing plans. The long-term plan to aim for is heaven. Ask what might God want in return for what talents have been given; who needs your special abilities; and what capabilities does God want you to acquire? Remember God wants an account for our lives. Looking back at life's end reminds us that life is intended to be meaningful with each one blessed with a unique purpose to serve God.

Construct a four-year plan with one-year objectives. Starting with some vision of life goals, construct a four-year plan. Formulating plans makes it easier to stay on track always working toward goals. Plans brace us against unpredictable winds and help us to bounce back when we get derailed. The next step is to construct goals within an even more manageable time frame, monthly, with tangible accomplishments that will be attained. Each goal activity comes with the chance to do the best we can do, and be the best we can be, in accordance with the gifts and expectations God has given us. At the end of each year, reassess, look at what was accomplished, then revise the four year and next year's plans as needed.

Plan with Family as a High Priority. Sometimes, one simply loses track of what should be most important to us, family. Those closest to us are often taken for granted.

Too much isolated overtime work, business travel, golf, softball, spectator sports can easily diminish the bonds of mutual respect and love. Being mentally removed is just as much an issue as being physically removed. Anything that prevents one from being with family and loved ones should be reexamined.

In today's fast-paced society, spouses race here and there, going from one place to another, without time to focus on each other, and even when together, their minds are racing past one other. Human relations require communication, mental connectivity, and emotional bonds that enable full openness and availability to one another. This means losing oneself and one's selfish pursuits in exchange for appreciation for family and personal peace. Understanding, forgiveness, unconditional love and respect are critical in marriage and for family. The problems of one's spouse or one's child affect the entire family. Sharing a mutual love for God as a family is the key to keeping the family strong and mutually supporting.

Implementation

Be open to modifications. Know that God can call at any time and change one's entire planned approach. Sometimes we think we have it all straight…then we get a real zinger and must change everything. Most certainly, plans rarely are implemented exactly as planned. As God's children, our purpose is always to be ready to respond as His call. The more we realize we are His, the simpler is life and less one is frustrated when things are uncontrollable. Being ready for change requires trust in the Lord. This served St. Francis of Assisi well, who rightly concluded that the pursuit of material things is passing. King Solomon, however, lamented on his deathbed that life was meaningless because he could not bring his great wealth with him once he had passed on. So don't lose sight of true needs and clearly, adjustments may be needed at any time as God's immediate plan supersedes our plans and objectives.

Don't worry about what you can't control. God always wants us to do our best, be alert and responsive to His call, energized to do all that one is called upon to do. If we follow this, we cannot be really concerned about the outcome, because the results and others' reactions are beyond our control. Remember, God is the only one who counts.

Mother Theresa said it simply: "God does not ask us to be successful, but to be faithful." Thus, we must trust the Holy Spirit to help us with the effort, but then leave it to Him to bring about whatever God wants from it. Often, we are only asked to plant a seed, though we may never see the fruits of it. It is not necessary to know now, it will be revealed in Heaven. For now, it is up to us to simply do our best as His instruments, and not look back. We don't need any thanks; it will be good enough to get the full picture later.

Your efforts count. Everyone is important in God's eyes, and He has a plan for each of us. Our time is on loan from God, so we need to make the most of it. Above all, "not knowing the day or hour" when we will be called to Him, we need to offer our time here always to God and to give honor to Him in all one does. Since we innately know that we live and breathe to be pleasing in God's eyes, it is not enough for our lives to just suffice. We are given life to pursue excellence through God's grace and support. When we forget, or are lazy, or run off track of that pursuit, we sense the loss of God's presence.

When we are not as productive as we can be, may have become distracted or side-tracked, it never feels right. If we could have done better, if we are not doing what is right for God, no one else may notice, but we know, and we know He knows.

God sees us through every task. God never gives us a job that we cannot accomplish if we have included Him in our plans and our implementation. No matter how large or small the task, significant or insignificant the job, we strive to do the best we can because it reflects on the One who created us…and He guides us along the way. Doing one's best in a business environment can be affected by the size, policy, and managerial style of the organization, as well as one's position within the organization. The larger the organization and the more authoritarian its management, the more conforming and efficient behavior is demanded to be. Smaller organizations with more democratic management give individuals more flexibility and a greater sense of achieving organizational goals in an individualistically expressive manner. Doing one's best may require very different responses in each type of environment, but regardless, it is achievable because a focus on true needs will always lead to the appropriate response in any situation.

Focus on the essential, trust, and let go. In sports, as in all of life, one's best performance emerges when self-distractions and self-centeredness disappears, and instead of forcing effort, one turns to relaxed and focused concentration, and lets go of self-consciousness. It is the same with every endeavor in life. Once we learn to let go of our selfish interest and strive to put our trust in God and let Him guide us, we will find our best performance.

Sometimes being the best one can be happens naturally because these principles become engaged even without one's awareness. A timid high school girl with few friends, for example, may become the spark of positive influence in a college where she knows no one. A family moves into a new neighborhood and finds one or more children have made significant improvements in their personality. A person long fearful of public speaking can mysteriously at mid-life, mature by losing self-concern and become an extremely effective and enthusiastic public speaker. Letting go of emotional concerns of others' opinions can produce new awakenings and major breakthroughs and accomplishments become possible.

Don't leave God behind. We should never go forward in the morning of our day without God. Even with the best intentions of doing our best, even when we are meeting self-actualization goals, it is like a man who goes out into a freezing snowstorm without a coat. Without God, problems can begin suddenly that snowball into much worse matters.

Just as there is a breakthrough point for the achievement of self-actualization, there is also a negative breakdown point where behavior can change markedly for the worse. Some examples are the hitter who goes into a horrendous slump; a star pitcher whose career is threatened when suddenly he can't seem to throw strikes; or the worker who encounters a continuous bombardment of stresses causing them to shut down and become numb and uncommunicative. Without the ability to turn to God, because of lack of belief or a feeling of isolation from separation, one's problems are difficult to resolve.

In the process of planning to be the best one can be, and in striving for self-actualization, we need to remember the higher goal, of seeking first the Kingdom of God. Whether God is involved in these activities is based on one's mental awareness and perceived purpose, and the personal benefit to others represented by the action. Life is a continuous adjustment process but consistent prayer, and the right thoughts, words, and deeds, will produce good ends. It is the quest, not necessarily the actual achievement that draws us closer to God, to neighbor, and the true fulfillment of self. Striving to make the most of one's capabilities to be as productive, effective, and successful as possible is part of the quest.

Develop an attitude of gratitude. Having the right attitude is very important for implementing any plan, as

Charles Swindoll[18] notes:

> "The longer I live, the more I realize the impact of attitude on life. Attitude, to me is more important than facts. It is more important than the past, than education, than money, than circumstances, than failures, than successes, than what other people think or say or do. It is more important than appearance, giftedness or skill. It will make or break a company...a church...a home. The remarkable thing is we have a choice every day regarding the attitude we will embrace for that day. We cannot change our past...we cannot change the fact that people will act in a certain way. We cannot change the inevitable. The only thing we can do is play on the one string we have, and that is our attitude. I am convinced that life is 10% what happens to me and 90% how I react to it. And so, with you...we are in charge of our attitudes."

The right will is motivated with humility and gratitude. Melody Beattie[19] remarks:

> "Gratitude unlocks the fullness of life. It turns what we have into enough, and more. It turns denial into acceptance, chaos to order, and

---

[18] Quote from a poster with attribute to Charles Swindoll. (Also see: C. Swindoll, *Living Above the Level of Mediocrity*, W Publishing, 1990.)

[19] M. Beattie, *Codependent No More*. San Francisco: Harper/Hazelden, 1987.

confusion to clarity. It turns a meal into a feast,
a house into a home, a stranger into a friend.
Gratitude makes sense of our past, brings peace
for today, and creates a vision for tomorrow."

Gratitude forms the attitude to fully and powerfully
implement God's plans for our lives.

Chapter 6

Facing the Fear of Dying

The most frightening thing about life is facing the final fact of life, that of dying. It is enough to put fear into anyone who dares to think about it. It is why some people give up once they become depressed and do not care about going on living. It is why others simply block the whole notion of dying completely out of one's mind almost for their entire lives.

Often a counselor hears the comment, "Why should I care about living when I am just going to die someday anyway?" Sure, dying is inevitable but God made us to be alive and to live life fully. There is no need to get depressed about dying; and why rush it, it will come when it is due. "We never know the day or the hour." (Matthew 25:13) In the meantime, we should try to be the best reflection of He who made us.

For the most part of life, death is not much of a conscious thought. It is there in the background and kept there, being almost inconceivable that it might someday apply to us. Why dwell on it; that only brings depression to most who do. Not until perhaps one's age reaches the mid-60s does it begin to sink in, that is, that the reality of the end of this life is indeed real. During one's earlier years, it is seen from time to time in the loss of parents, of close friends or relatives, or in time of war, or in the daily reporting of the sad stories that appear in the nightly news. Still, one tends not to spend much time personalizing it, thinking about it as it applies to oneself.

The truth is that the mind blocks serious thought about one's own final days. It is often not until Old Man Death makes a strong case in its favor during a serious illness or accident that one begins to understand clearly and personally how truly inevitable it is. When in good health, one does not worry about it or fear it in an abnormal way at any age. Remember, every breath we have is a gift and our last one is our soul's first breath of divine life as a reward for a life well lived. This is our hope.

The best way to think about death is to just always trust in God. Throughout the dying process, which is a real part of life, God is there keeping us close to Him, and when our time is up, He will be there to bring us into a new more glorious eternal life. That is, it's natural to fear dying because we love life. For those who live their life with gusto for the love of God, they have a special place reserved with Him that they intuitively long to be as well. They go from their "Heaven on Earth" to the real thing, whatever that is exactly no one knows, but again, we can trust in Him that it is better than we can imagine and know that Jesus is the proof of this.

The Last Days

A popular name in the subject of "death and dying" is the author, Elisabeth Kübler-Ross whose 1969 book, *On Death and Dying*,[20] has become a classic, accepted model

---

[20] Elisabeth Kübler-Ross, *On Death & Dying*, (Simon & Schuster/Touchstone), 1969.

for understanding the stages of grieving for the person with terminal illness as well as their loved ones. The five stages are:

- *denial,*
- *anger,*
- *bargaining,*
- *depression and*
- *acceptance.*

The stages have a certain universal appeal even though the author admits that such a range of emotions or the exact sequence of them is not felt by everyone, some only experience as few as two of the emotions. She adds that they also may be generalized to many areas of life where there is any type of personal loss or rejection (e.g., loss of job, income, relationship, etc.).

There are a variety of questions that come to mind when examining each of the five stages. For example, it would seem the stage of *"denial"* can be expected until doctors provide clear evidence of tests. For who would believe a fateful diagnosis particularly if the symptoms do not seem to present such a fateful outcome?

Then if given sufficient proof, *"anger"* does not always result unless a person feels it is unfair and they are unlucky. It seems the difference in reaction is one between the emotional mind and the logical mind, where the first is an immediate reaction and the latter is a thoughtful understanding regardless of the lack of reason on the cause of the illness.

Similarly, if one cannot claim responsibility for bringing on the illness, how does the *"bargaining"* stage proceed? That is, how does one negotiate with God for a healing in exchange for good behavior, if their behavior has not been even a partial cause for the problem? Then also, how does one negotiate with God if they don't or won't believe in God?

For anyone who doesn't believe in God, certainly *"depression"* is a natural response, for the person sees little hope in the future, as they don't believe in Heaven and the soul's eternity. Certainly, for anyone with a terminal illness, however, where time is of the essence, it will be important to tie up loose ends and say goodbye to loved ones and thus, one becomes somewhat reclusive knowing that their end may be swift. This is not depression but should be considered making the best of one's time to bring about a logical constructive conclusion to one's life.

Then there is the matter of acceptance. Does the person need to "give up and give in" for there to be *"acceptance?"* What if the individual fights until the end, fights to live another breath and at the same time accepts the likely inevitable outcome? It seems both are possible at the same time, struggling to stay alive, hoping for a miracle, but submitting if it be God's will.

Whether the personal struggle with death proceeds more smoothly for individuals who experience the full range of emotions or stays in the denial or the depression stage to the end depends on the individual. Maybe the primary difference on how people face death needs to include one's thoughts and beliefs on God, and on their own meaning of life and death. The following two sections attempt to address this aspect regarding the stages of death and dying, particularly as an aid to those struggling with fear, anger, and depression.

Job's Response in the Old Testament

In Mike Mazzalongo's article "*A Christian's Response to Death and Dying*,"[21] he explains that:

> "as a human being, a believer's response to his/her own terminal illness or the death of a loved one is the same as any other person's response. However, because of faith in God and trust in Christ, that response goes beyond the mere five steps that Kübler-Ross described."

The author describes the Biblical story of Job, who was "wealthy and well respected in his community for his goodness, wisdom and piety; had a large family of sons and daughters, and who God permitted Satan to test him to see if he would be faithful in trial through many losses as he had been in abundance, including the loss of his wealth, children, health, reputation, and the love and support of his wife and his family."

The author describes how Job responded citing the 5 steps below that Job went through in his experience with death and dying (the following pages are selected excerpts

---

[21] Mike Mazzalongo, "A Christian's Response to Death and Dying." Bible Talk post. Jan 11, 2015.

from his insightful book):

Step #1 – Mourning:
"Then Job arose and tore his robe and shaved his head" - Job 1:20.

Job immediately begins to lament the loss of his children as well as the other good things he had enjoyed for so long. Note that he accepts as true the events that have befallen him. That he tears his robe, shaves his head and falls to the ground are natural human and cultural responses to these tragedies. What Job did was the normal and healthy way to deal with tragedy: lamenting and mourning.

In some cultures, family members wear black for a year after the death of a close relative. This is a good way to separate oneself for a time of spiritual, emotional and social renewal. In effect it says: "Don't mind me, I'm in mourning." The worse detriment to recovery from a tragedy is to force a time limit for ourselves to "get over" our loss. If you don't weep and mourn when it happens, you'll weep and mourn later. Many depressions and anxieties are the result of improper time and effort given over to mourning the loss of a loved one, marriage, health or family situation. Mourning was all Job could do at this point, and he did it as a way of saving his sanity.

Step #2 – Worship:
"And he fell to the ground and worshiped. He

said, "Naked I came from my mother's womb, and naked I shall return there. The Lord gave and the Lord has taken away. Blessed be the name of the Lord." - Job 1:20b-21

As a believer, once Job could struggle to right himself from the shock, his first thought is to go to God in worship and prayer. It is unfortunate that so many see prayer as a last hope, a grasping at straws when things go wrong. Instead of worship, tragedy leads many to drink and do drugs; excessively eat or abuse of themselves in various ways; and do all kinds of escapist methods to deal with the great pain associated with death and dying. Of course, the verse here in Job does not contain all that he said, doesn't repeat for us every prayer uttered; rather we are given the conclusion of his worship and talking to God. We read about the insight that he first gains as a result of that prayer.

Initial prayer and worship do not always produce such deep insights into the nature of our situation and such clarity about its meaning. However, when the thought of existing one more minute on this earth is too painful to bear - the only place we can and should go is to God in humble worship and prayer. If trouble, pain and death don't drive us to our knees, what will?

It's like being strapped into a roller coaster where we feel powerless to affect anything happening to us or to our feelings. For this reason, we need to come closer to the one who does have the power to control all things - including death. This may not change the circumstances, but it does bring us peace and, at times, a certain understanding. Job did this, and although his situation did not change, through his tears he was rewarded with a crystal-clear understanding of the true nature of his life and its ultimate meaning and substance.

Step #3 – Silence:
"Through all this Job did not sin nor did he blame God." - Job 1:22

Although later Job did break his silence, his first and correct impulse was to hold his peace, contemplate his situation and wait upon the Lord. The Bible explains this by saying that Job didn't complain to or blame God. He didn't charge God foolishly. He didn't question God as to the timing, the fairness or the degree of his suffering. He didn't dwell on the "why" of it all with the suggestion that there may have been a better way, an easier way. He did not substitute a plan of his own for what had happened that might have lessened the blow. He said nothing concerning the events and how they took place.

The Bible says that in doing this, he sinned not. Kübler-Ross described the stages of grieving as denial, anger, bargaining, depression and acceptance. We've come to see these as the normal human progression and response to death and dying. We should also note that for a weak and sinful person these may be normal responses, however, to lash out at God in anger; to question His actions; and to try and change His decision or feel sorry for ourselves; these are fleshly, worldly responses born out of our sinful and weak natures. The only spiritual reaction is the final stage, the one of acceptance. *(The author means the very final stage.)*

Compare these however, with Job's initial response to death and dying where he mourned and lamented his loss. We see that within his very first reaction, is included most of Kübler-Ross' normal human responses of denial, anger and depression. Then Job drew near to God in prayer and worship. He didn't bargain with God, he bowed down before God in humility and trust. Then Job remained silent. During this time, he contemplated his situation and searched for meaning. Eventually he developed a life-threatening illness, lost the support of his wife and was condemned by his friends as a sinner who had brought all this misery upon himself. These additional burdens led Job to the last two steps in the believer's journey through the experience of grief and dying.

Step #4 - Enlightenment
For nearly 40 chapters in an on-going

dialogue with his friends we watch Job as he comes to grips with not simply the reality and meaning of his suffering but the truth that stands behind not only his suffering but the suffering of all men. Job learns that his experience is worth it if it reveals more perfectly the God he believes in. In other words, if your suffering serves to give you a glimpse of God Almighty, then it is a small matter and any complaining was foolish and sinful in comparison to what has been discovered, what has been given to you.

Enlightenment, especially that enlightenment that enables us to see God more clearly is of more value than what we have lost - whatever that is, however we suffer.   Job learned that life as well as death is in God's hands and the painful experience of it is justified if it leads us face to face with God, even if it's for a moment. That one moment is worth all the suffering. The non-believers' best hope is to arrive at that point where they accept reality and learn to cope with it. That reality being that people suffer and die and there is nothing they can do about it except carry on as best they can - this is as good as it gets!

Suffering and death for believers, however, bring them face to face with the ultimate reality that there is a living God who gives life and controls death by His power. The ultimate end therefore is that death and dying can serve to strengthen faith and hope, and consequently loosen the grip of fear and sorrow that these experiences have on our hearts. Only an enlightened person like Paul the Apostle could write these words when facing death. For to me to live is Christ, and to die is gain- Philippians 1:21. Paul had seen beyond suffering and death and had a glimpse of God's reality, and this vision was worth all the suffering he had to endure.

Step #5 - Restoration
In the last chapter we learn that God heals Job and restores his family, wealth and position. This didn't change the fact that Job had suffered and lost children and prestige; his suffering was real. You see, God doesn't give us our old lives back; He gives us a new life. Here on earth, it is a life we can live and live with. Sometimes it is very different. Sometimes it is harder. But for believers, it is always a life where God is more prominent than before.

In the end, He is the reward for persevering. You may not have a parent, child, spouse, loved one or health anymore, but you now have more of Him to make up for it. And in the next world, the great promise for those who have experienced the enlightenment of suffering is that you will have all of Him all the time because after your death you will leave behind everything that comes between you and Him now.[22]

Another Model of the Dying Process

A faithful individual, one who believes in God, when facing death and dying, approaches their terminal illness in the following sequential steps or stages:

1. ***Hopes for the best but immediately finds a priest to seek repentance from all sins, known and unknown, realized and unrealized, through the "anointing of the sick" and the "Apostolic Pardon" for the remission of the temporal punishment due to sin.*** The individual first hopes their illness is not terminal. This is not a denial of the truth. It is hoping for the best while taking immediate action to repent and rectify any last known offenses against God and man.

2. ***Resolves to fight for their life.*** After all the facts are in and upon realizing the prognosis is true, the individual resolves to do all they can to fight it with whatever drugs or other strategies that might work, however low the probability of success.

3. ***Prays for a miracle.*** A person of faith will pray to God for a miraculous intervention and call upon all their heavenly and earthly intercessors for prayer in this regard.

---

[22] Ibid.

4. ***Prays for courage and help with the suffering, and to offer the pain up for the reparation of sins of oneself, family, and the world.*** While the prayer for healing continues, at the same time a prayer begins to develop for the courage to put one's entire trust in God for whatever is meant to be. This prayer calls for God's help with the suffering, to be able to endure it.

5. ***Considers the future of one's family and closest friends and gives proper notice of any practical last details to be carried out especially regarding their children an loved ones.*** The prayer evolves into asking for help to prepare oneself to meet their Savior in person and for being ready to let go.

6. ***Prays for the acceptance of letting go of this life and to be able to go confidently into the next life. Practical planning for one's own funeral may even take place.*** This prayer grows to include God's help for the care of one's family in the immediate and long-term future.

In this respect, the faithful person proceeds through stages of the physical and spiritual that correspond to one's advancing illness and decline. As the inevitable end becomes more obvious, the prayer corresponds to the greater needs at hand. That is, what becomes relevant are the last things, the final judgement, as the prayers of hope for a miraculous recovery diminish. The faith filled death and dying process does eventually lead to an "acceptance" stage.

In the acceptance stage, the prayer puts one's trust in God to take care of one's family and all the responsibilities this individual, when healthy, took care of. This letting go of one's responsibilities, giving of them over to others and to God to sort out, comes just before the ultimate stage, that of letting go of life itself. This final stage is the last step in this life and the first in the next. It is hopefully a homecoming to an eternity that begins with a welcomed uniting with Jesus, Mary and Joseph, and the waiting arms of God, the Father, who created us, and the Holy Spirit that sustained and guided us through this life.

Thus, the five emotional stages of Kubler Ross: denial, anger, bargaining, **depression** and acceptance, may all come into play for the one facing a terminal diagnosis, but they will be experienced a bit differently if one has faith. For believers in God, the first four stages may be experienced temporarily but will not be given so much time and energy or the level of emotional intensity, such as becoming stuck in fear, anger, and depression, as might be the case for non-believers.

For non-believers, the last stage as well, the acceptance phase, is likely to be experienced very differently. For non-believers, as one accepts their personal end, there is nothing to look forward to, and their only peace comes from whatever love surrounds them, and whatever legacy they fondly think about as they say goodbye.

For believers in God, the natural fear and depression is overcome by trust and hope in God. This last stage can even be a chance to think about what Heaven is all about, how their every unanswered question is answered as one discovers every knowledge that human awareness could never realize. It is the ultimate reuniting with family going back to generations one never knew. It is a time to find old friends who left this world too soon or to explore what good may have come from some seed one may have planted (i.e., some emotional, social, intellectual, or material support given to another). That is, it is a time to see how many souls you may have touched in your life, and how much good you did and so much more that a human mind cannot even imagine. For the faithful, it is the arrival of a lifelong waiting for the ultimate fulfillment that words cannot begin to describe, but above all, it is a sense one can leave this great life on earth and go in peace and joy to God and to an existence that is infinitely greater than here on Earth.

Bibliography

AA World Services. *Alcoholics Anonymous*. NY: Alcoholics Anonymous World Services, 1939.

Alberti R.E., Emmons M.L., *Your Perfect Right*, San Lius Obispo, CA: Impact, 1974.

American Psychiatric Association's *Diagnostic and Statistical Manual of Mental Disorders*, Fourth Edition, Text Revision, 2000.

Beattie M., *Codependent No More*. San Francisco: Harper/Hazelden, 1987.

Christensen, Carl, Dawn Farm Education Series: Wayne State University School of Medicine, 2011.

From the Voice, "Addiction: A brain disease with biological underpinnings." Hazelden publications, 2001.

Kübler-Ross, Elisabeth, *On Death & Dying*, (Simon & Schuster/Touchstone), 1969.

Luft, J., "The Johari Window," Human Relations and Training News, Jan 1961.

Mazzalongo, Mike, "A Christian's Response to Death and Dying." Bible Talk, Jan 2015.

Pope Benedict XVI, Words from his inauguration Mass.

Swindoll C., *Living Above the Level of Mediocrity*, W Publishing, 1990.)

The Harvard Mental Health Letter, "The Addicted Brain." July 2004.

The National Institute of Mental Health (NIMH) website, posted Aug 2018.

Torres G, Horowitz JM (1999). "Drugs of abuse and brain gene expression". *Psychosom Med.* 61 (5): 630–50.

Bill W. and Dr. Bob, *The Big Book, Alcoholics Anonymous*. Alcoholics Anonymous World Services. 1939 (original version).

* 9 7 8 1 7 2 6 2 3 8 4 1 0 *